THE OPEN CURRICULUM

PALMETTO
PUBLISHING
Charleston, SC
www.PalmettoPublishing.com

The Open Curriculum
Copyright © 2023 by Marlene Rellinger Chapin

Cover art provided by pexels.com>/@maksim-mihno

mcilluminations@gmail.com

Paperback ISBN: 979-8-8229-2415-4

THE OPEN CURRICULUM

A GUIDE TO EVALUATING STUDENT PORTFOLIOS

Marlene Rellinger Chapin

NBCT/EAYA

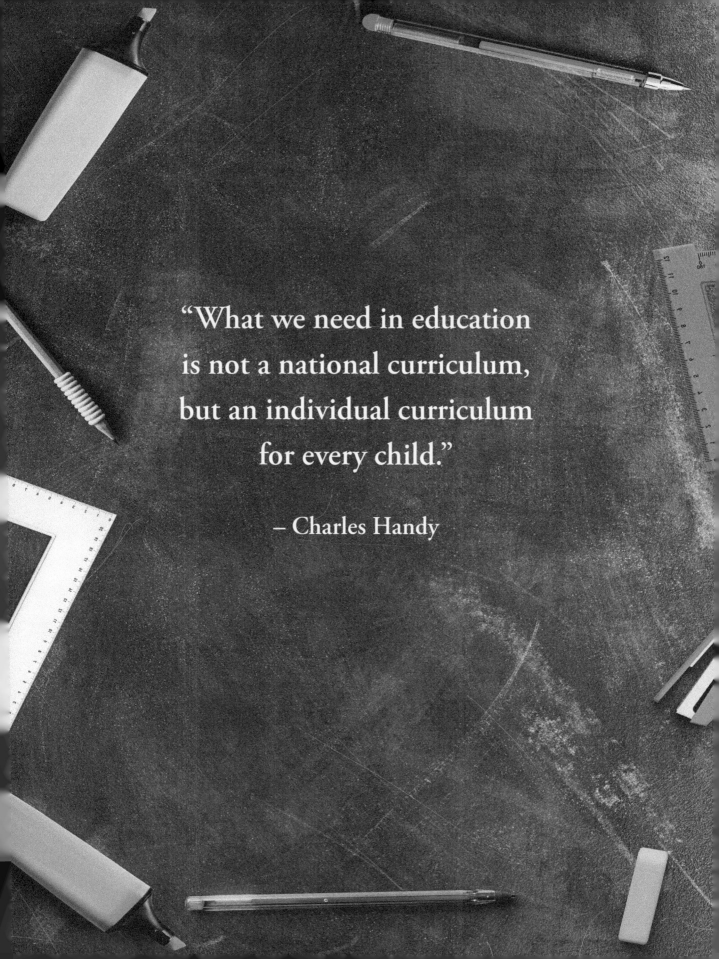

"What we need in education
is not a national curriculum,
but an individual curriculum
for every child."

– Charles Handy

In Loving Memory
of
Paige Foster

We miss you, still do…
walking through these halls,
narrow paths of footprints
following the crowds.
Too soon you tried to break away,
before you could sustain
the weight of such a world,
its promises and pain.
Here is what I dreamt for you,
and what the world had meant for you.

ACKNOWLEDGMENTS

I want to express my deep appreciation for the dedicated teachers in Pennsylvania, Ohio, and Wisconsin. Their commitment to the creative development of children and teens kept me writing for over twenty years. I am especially grateful to friends, colleagues, and administrators: Dr. David Axner, Dr. Dale Carlton, Dr. Lynn Catlin, Donna Corsi, Rebecca Diener, Barb Dougal, Dr. Edie Holcomb, David King, Norma Madsen, Toni Jill Rieger, Dr. Steven Schroeder, Dr. James Trusso, and Chris VanderArk for their valuable input and support. Special thanks to Palmetto Publishing and statistician Dr. J. Bardales for their professional expertise.

Above all, I want to express further appreciation to my husband—Dale—for his patient prodding and collaboration, my children—Daniel, Stephanie, and Johanna—for their endless encouragement, and my grandchildren—Noah, Madeline, and Luca—who I pray will never lose their incredible imaginations. I would like to also mention my parents—Arthur and Doris (Rayman) Rellinger—and my six siblings—Karla, David, Howard, Tina, Toni Jill, and Douglas—who taught me many of these lessons a lifetime ago. Lastly, in memory of AJ, our beloved boxer who warmed my feet with unconditional love to the end.

PREFACE

This book is a final goodbye to my students, whom I owe a lifetime of learning. It is a welcome to future art educators with whom I will journey long after these pages fade. You must know that art education is a bit of an oxymoron: kids versus the curriculum, individuality standing against conformity. It is no wonder why the arts continue to fight for equality with core curricular domains. Still, the climb is invigorating! Every mountaintop experience becomes a plateau when the fog lifts. You, as I now, will stop somewhere along the way to encourage those with the heart and stamina to climb beyond. My teaching career is over, but if yours is just beginning, here are my takeaways:

- Students can control tools and materials, inventing technique, so you can *give permission*.
- Students can define problems in their work and risk making mistakes, so you can *defer judgment*.
- Students can recognize their own ideas and express a personal connection with subject matter, so you can *trust them*.
- Students can reflect upon meaning and communicate with others through their work, so you can *provide feedback*.
- Students can deconstruct and reconstruct their work over time, so you can *document their growth*.
- Students can follow a line of inquiry through multiple works that achieve curricular goals, so you can *evaluate them*.
- Students can transcend curriculum creating work that adds novelty to the previous historical works of others, so you can finally *retire*.

Curriculum is a living, fluid catalyst for growth in the hands of our youth. It can promote autonomy and initiative. The greatest gift we can offer our students is the freedom to exercise their innate, intrinsic motivation to learn. Extrinsic motivation for grades or teacher approval are ends unto themselves. Throughout my thirty-year career, however, grades rarely told the story of an individual student's growth. More often, curricular objectives evaluate individuals in comparison with peers in the same classroom setting. In this book you will learn that it is possible to teach a rigorous curriculum unencumbered by grading dozens of assignments to prove your instruction is fair and equitable. We cling to the mistaken belief that only intelligence that is tested can be taught. Nothing could be farther from the truth.

TABLE OF CONTENTS

INTRODUCTION

As a twice National Board Certified Teacher in EAYA (Early Adolescence through Young Adulthood Art) you may think that I would feel a sense of accomplishment. Not yet. For every positive influence on one student, I recall making mistakes with others. Some of those mistakes are still painful, including Paige Foster to whom this book is dedicated. Nearly invisible, Paige stealthily lands in the back row of my art room. Delicate strawberry wisps of hair pull away from her ponytail. In black couture, Paige neither speaks nor makes eye contact with anyone. I watch her explore various art materials until our eyes meet, and a smile curls out of her lips. The tools and materials in the art room resonate with Paige, connecting her with something intrinsically felt, a sense of belonging.

Paige's early pieces in the semester are usually in charcoal or black craypa. She depicts a figure fighting a storm (1) and someone sitting distant and alone on a bench (2).

Figure 1   Figure 2

As Paige works in successive pieces, she expresses feelings about school. She represents school as a long hallway with a dead end (3). Then the hallways have an exit, walking past childhood drawings leading to an opening of light and color (4). Her memories are reshaping the present. At this point my inner art teacher takes over. I begin documenting curricular standards for the elements of art and principles of design. She uses line and shape to create depth in the picture plane. A range of values are evident in the work, from darks to mediums to lights. Color also begins to emerge through the choice of pastels instead of charcoal. But the most significant growth that I observe is the change in her behavior. Paige demonstrates confidence in her ability to express personal thoughts and feelings. She moves to the middle of the room spreading out her work onto adjacent table spaces. Paige recognizes that peers in the classroom see her as an artist. She *thinks* like a visual artist. Traditional assignments are from a teacher who chooses the subject matter and the medium of expression for students. But the personal reflection and intrinsic motivation that Paige exhibits through her own choices is a deeper level of learning.

Figure 3

Figure 4

The hallways give way to open spaces, and a figure emerges (5). Light sources appear to help us see that the figure has a shadow (6). Planes begin to overlap, creating more movement throughout her work. The growth in Paige's portfolio of work documents her personal journey through depression. She remembers childhood as a happier time. Her art takes us on a journey, forward and backward, like a pendulum, reconciling past experiences with future hopes and dreams. Paige is expressing her sadness and loss of innocence through this portfolio of work.

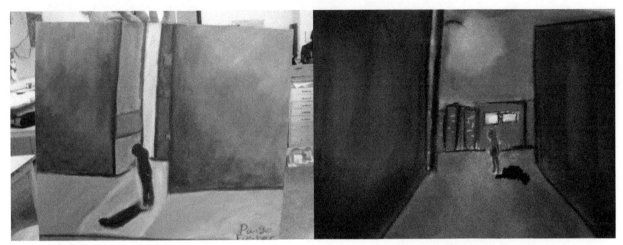

Figure 5   Figure 6

I first met Paige during the spring semester of 2011. Before leaving for the summer, she started a new piece that had a tiny green vine growing from the bottom edge. One small leaf unfurling upward was defying the ominous dark branches above it. Paige had a growth mindset. Unfortunately, she could not schedule an art class for the fall semester of that year. I was looking forward to seeing her again in the spring of 2012. Tragically, on November 1, 2011, she took her own life. Nothing can prepare you for the untimely loss of a student. No curriculum, no methodologies, no rubrics for evaluation will help you navigate the social media bullying and isolation many students feel at school. I will always wonder if an art class that fall semester could have changed her mind. In my dream for Paige, she would skip over the colored chalk in her drawings to young adulthood, leaving the dark shadows behind. I now comprehend, too late, what is eerily prescient in her work.

Thousands of teenagers pass through our school hallways looking for a reflection of themselves in the world and find no mirror. Often students have class schedules that do not address their individual needs. We fit kids into curriculum, rather than fitting curriculum around the kids. According to the World Health Organization, depression is the leading cause of illness and disability among adolescents

(WHO, 2021) and suicide is the third leading cause of death between the ages of fifteen through nineteen years. Teenagers are at a crossroads, looking for an identity that recognizes their strengths, where they will find success. Our failure to provide such opportunities for all students can lead them to addictions and self-harming behaviors. We are failing students in one basic need—the sense of belonging.

Kathleen "Paige" Foster
1994-2011

CHAPTER ONE

Kids vs. Curriculum

My search is for a model of curriculum that can document a student's intrinsic motivation to learn. Testing and grading policies measure a student's extrinsic motivation for achieving rewards or avoiding punishments. As such, evaluation remains *outside* the control of many students. Even Common Core standards facilitate a top-down curricular paradigm that relies heavily on standardized testing (Superville, 2015). When those extrinsic rewards coincide with the intrinsic motivation of the student, behaviors and outcomes are authentic because the interests and preferences of a student align with curriculum. This is student *engagement*, one of those oxymorons in education. You cannot teach it. Yet students do not retain learning without it. Engagement happens because something resonates within a student that ignites their interests and motivates them. Learning is wired into our human DNA, but not every student will find success in school. Our evaluation tools have become archaic, too focused on a narrow view of intelligence. As a result, many students fail to engage or simply detach from their own intrinsic motivation to learn. The educational doors of opportunity are closing around them.

Diane Ravitch (2013) calls the cultural shift toward extrinsic rewards in education the "Reign of Error" controlling curriculum through school funding. Specifically, the idea of school funding is based on how each student performs on standardized tests. Standardized testing became mandatory with the *No Child Left Behind Act* (NCLB) in 2002. Previously, the *National Assessment of Educational Progress* (NAEP) gathered information through random test sampling. They were used for diagnostic purposes at the federal, state and local district levels. Not every student was required to test, and no student names were attached to the reports. *Every Student Succeeds Act* (ESSA) replaced NCLB in 2015 and removed the federal funding penalty, but standardized testing continues to target individuals by school district. This paradigm is based on inequality because if someone succeeds, someone else must fail.

Testing has become a panacea for the growing uncertainty we feel from vast flooding of information into curricular areas. We may even be *creating* achievement gaps through the biases inherent in comparing students through a uniform test (Kendi, 2016). Even more foreboding is an Austrian born art educator's warning… "Having experienced the devastating effects of rigid dogmatism and disrespect for individual differences, I know that force does not solve problems and that the basis for human relationships is usually created in the homes and kindergartens. I feel strongly, that without the imposed discipline common in German family lives and schools, the acceptance of totalitarianism would have been impossible" (Lowenfeld, 1952). An open curriculum, where students choose how they will demonstrate course requirements by following their interests and intrinsic motivation to learn, can correct those errors.

One day in October, I decided to explore intrinsic motivation, looking for clues about how and when children become self-conscious, hesitant in making their own art. The kindergarten students are holding hands and giggling as they walk into the art room. They quickly find their table and sit on the edge of their chairs so they can easily pivot. Next to each table is a cart full of art materials, chalks, crayons, markers, colored pencils, and craypas. On each table are blank pieces of white drawing paper, 12 by 18 inches. Within minutes every student chooses their favorite medium and begins drawing. I stand at the front of the room in amazement. No instruction is given. There are no directions to follow. No one asks how I am grading them. They already *know* what to do.

Walking around the room, I observe that their choices of subject matter and medium are different. How do they know what to draw? Quite simply they are drawing what they are thinking about, demonstrating an awareness of their own thoughts and feelings. In addition, these young students are choosing a material to represent those mental images. Connecting an imaginary idea with a material in real space is where intrinsic motivation becomes "choice" or "preference." When students doodle, or brainstorm ideas in a journal or sketchbook, and sometimes on the back of their hands, they are responding to personal thoughts and giving them recognition. The early drawings of childhood are excellent examples of intrinsic motivation at work.

When the next class of first graders arrive, the story is quite different. They come to art class in a straight and quiet line. The students file in one by one and sit in their assigned seats with all the seriousness they can muster. As they enter, I stand at the front of the room smiling. Paper lies on each table and art materials are on a cart next to the tables. The students sit quietly, looking at me and waiting. I continue smiling in response. Several minutes pass before one brave student begins to reach for the materials on a cart. "You can't do that!" a classmate says urgently. "You have to wait for the teacher."

Embarrassingly, the student raises his hand and asks, "Can I use the crayons?"

"Yes," I reply.

A few more minutes pass, then another student asks, "What about the markers?"

I nod, showing my approval.

Before long all the first graders are doing *exactly* what the kindergarteners demonstrated in the previous period. It is not that they are unaware of their thoughts and feelings. None of them appear unclear about what to draw. But in one year's time the first graders are more field-dependent. They learn what is socially and culturally appropriate, and that is to wait for directions and permission from a teacher. Their initial hesitance is simply the social behaviors of well-trained school age children. The educational environment is a powerful shaper of extrinsic motivation in students. It can restrain bodily kinesthetic movement and subsequent initiative, which further instills their fear of disapproval. Student engagement begins with trust in a teacher and classroom where making decisions, even mistakes, are evidence of learning. There is a reservoir of information *already* inside the students themselves. Their memories of past experiences are the context through which curriculum comes alive.

Student engagement is inherently personal. For example, Eric brings a drawing to me in colored craypas that was, by far, his best work. The warm colors are moving from lighter areas to cool shadows. There is spontaneity and playfulness in the drawing much like Eric himself. But he is not working on the classroom assignment. How do I grade him? I look around my classroom. Some students are working on the assignment, others working on choice-based projects after completing the assignment. But some students are checking their phones, chatting, getting to class late or missing class altogether. Eric usually joins his friends at the social circle. Studying his work, I realize that the portrait meets color requirements in the curriculum that I had yet to teach. Eric is watching and waiting. I was hesitant, but recovered saying, "Beautiful, keep working with color!"

Eric never completes my regular assignments. But his work in the spring art exhibit is *original* artwork. Students have much to teach us. I understand now that student engagement occurs when the extrinsic rewards/approval from a teacher *follows* evidence of intrinsic motivation from the students. The kids come first, not the curriculum. Over time, my assignments slowly became options, available for students to include in their choice-based work or to give them an exploratory activity while planning their next piece. Soon Eric's friends are creating choice-based projects of their own. Problem behaviors in the classroom decrease. Time spent on task, albeit not the same task at the same time, increases. The students are effectively and intuitively differentiating the art curriculum. Now I must learn how to evaluate the diverse outcomes.

All standards of evaluating student artwork involves evidence of the elements of art and the principles of design. But students are working on different assignments in an open curriculum. As a result, evidence of the elements of art and principles of design will be different for each student. For example, Eric's work begins with color and portraiture. His choice of medium is craypas, adding texture as well as color to his composition. In addition, he learns to create value by mixing complements to darken and desaturate his colors. Eric's choice of subject matter, a portrait, uses shallow space bringing the viewer closer to his subject. Emphasis is on the facial expressions with more detail in a focal area around the eyes. So how would you assess this piece? Chart One includes the rubrics that suggest scores for Eric's portrait. The rubric shows which elements of art and principles of design are evident in his drawing. Another student's work may score differently. The rubrics are flexible enough to evaluate students individually while looking for similar behaviors and artistic thinking processes.

The rubrics limit the elements of art to five, including line, shape, value, color, and texture (Ocvirk, Stinson 2006). The principles of design are also minimal for evaluation purposes including movement, repetition, balance, dominance, emphasis, and contrast. Both rubrics are "common assessments" because all students are evaluated by the same criteria. Rather than grading one product at a time, however, students earn points by demonstrating clear and consistent evidence from multiple pieces of work. This provides students with many opportunities to demonstrate their understanding and skills, as well as areas that need further exploration.

Student preferences may not seem important, but they provide the baseline for determining growth. After students make choices about subject matter and medium of expression, evidence of the elements and principles begin to emerge. From there, development in the work can be documented. The rubrics indicate consistency in the student work by recording *overall* growth. The same rubric allows students to improve their scores with future work. Regardless of their choices of medium or subject matter student work always demonstrates some evidence of the elements and principles. Another thing that I have noticed is that when a student is working on integrating a particular element or principle, they will let go of other elements and principles that were previously in their portfolio work. But when they gain control over the new element previous skills return to their work.

Evaluation, then, begins when students initiate a baseline work. It is from that product that subsequent work demonstrates progress. In the past, when everyone followed the same directions, grading was simply a comparison between students. But you will recognize a quality in choice-based student work that is authentic, ideas that you have never seen before, reflections and connections that are truly creative. Students also notice a difference in their work; it expresses something meaningful to them. Achievement in an open curriculum reflects the choices students make in their portfolio work. Following a student's thinking process will help you connect their work to the art curriculum. In fact, you will find that, while no one student is working on the same assignment, they each demonstrate proficiency in some area of the curriculum which can be documented.

Regarding supplies, the same budget is required for choice-based learning, provided class sizes remain consistent. However, instead of purchasing entire class sets of tools and materials, smaller numbers of each material available in the art room provides students with a wider variety of choices.

Chart One
Common Assessments for Visual Art
Summative Rubric for the Elements of Art

CRITERIA Elements of Art	Consistent Evidence	Clear Evidence	Some Evidence	Not Yet Evidence	Pts.
Element-Line	Lines are edges that depict the intersection of differing planes of value or color.	Intersecting/ overlapping lines that disappear and reappear moving up, down, right, left, forward, and backward in the picture plane.	Contour outlines and/or horizon lines.	No contour out-lines or horizon lines.	2
Element-Shape	Overlapping shapes creating multiple vertical planes behind the foreground plane.	Overlapping shapes to create an imaginary plane behind the foreground plane.	Geometric and/or free-form shape.	No obvious shapes.	2
Element-Value	Light, medium, and dark values from a direction-al or imaginary light source.	Gradations of lights through mediums and darks.	Light values and/or dark values.	No lights or darks.	2
Element-Color	Use of color value by adding complements with a hue that darkens and whites to lighten.	Use of color temperature (lights warmer and darks cooler using colors anal-ogous to hue).	Use of one or more colors, (warm and/ or cool).	No use of color.	4
Element-Texture	Implied tex-tures that also depict value rendering from a light source.	Implied textures (i.e., cross-hatch-ing, stip-ple, patterning).	Applied textures (i.e., printing, sgraffito, blend-ing, impasto).	No use of texture.	2
				TOTAL POINTS	

Grading scores, A 16-20, B 11-15, C 6-10, Insufficient evidence 1-5.

Summative Rubric for the Principles of Design

CRITERIA Principles of Design	Consistent Evidence	Clear Evidence	Some Evidence	Not Yet Evidence	Pts.
Movement creates Unity	Element appears in multiple vertical planes behind the foreground plane, establishing middle and backgrounds.	Element appears in a vertical plane behind the foreground plane, establishing a middle ground.	Element extends off the edges of the picture plane, defining an imaginary space.	Element is on a single vertical plane, no overlapping.	1
Repetition creates Unity	Element repeated in multiple vertical planes behind the foreground plane with overlapping.	Element repeated in a vertical plane behind the foreground plane with overlapping.	Element is repeated but on the same foreground plane with no overlapping.	Element not repeated in the picture plane.	2
Balance creates Unity	Lines of axes separating the composition into more than two intersecting planes.	Line of axis separating the composition into approximate halves, establishing two intersecting planes.	Radial balance around one or more focal points on the same foreground plane.	No organization to elements.	2
Dominance creates Variety	More than one element combines with another to create dominance (i.e., warm colors with organic shapes next to cool colors with angular shapes).	Dominant element in background and middle ground planes visually move to foreground.	Dominant element is repeated on one or more vertical planes (i.e., lines, shapes, values, colors, textures).	No elements dominant.	2

Emphasis creates Variety	Viewer can visually read the intention of the artist from the meaning in a focal area.	Viewer can interpret or visually read some meaning in a focal area.	Meaning attached to focal area but difficult to interpret or visually read.	No meaning attached to focal area.	2
Contrast creates Variety	Contrasting element(s) present within background, middle and foreground planes.	Contrasting element(s) present within middle and foreground planes.	Contrasting element(s) present (i.e., light vs. dark, warm vs. cool, angular vs. curvilinear) on a foreground plane.	No contrast present.	2
				TOTAL POINTS	

Grading scores, A 19-24, B 13-18, C 7-12, Insufficient evidence 1-6.

Another concern you may have regards the monitoring of a wide variety of tools and materials in an open curriculum. As you grow to understand the choices students make about materials and subject matter, the classroom environment is *more* manageable. In one class period several students may be working with clay or jewelry and others may be painting using watercolors, acrylics, and oils. Because the different materials involve a smaller number of students, not an entire class, monitoring is much easier than if all students were working with Exacto knives, for example. In addition, because many of the students will spend significant time mastering their choice of materials, their progress is clearly noticeable. A bonus occurs when in each studio class, kids learn that they have skills to help someone else just learning a new technique or subject matter. There's always someone you can learn from and others you can teach in a studio class. A culture of reciprocity and mutual interest in everyone's success fills the art room.

Terminology and skills also develop for different students at different rates. An open curriculum permits *students* to choose which elements and principles they will focus on throughout instruction. Any one piece within a portfolio that demonstrates improvement in consistency will raise a student's score. In addition, student scores are banked. There is no going backwards on the rubrics. Students are not losing points, starting over with each new piece as with curricular assignments from a teacher. They are always moving forward horizontally on the rubrics towards mastery, or vertically as they incorporate new elements and principles to broaden their skills.

Chart Two is a student's checklist for the elements of art and principles of design found in no more than ten *chronological* pieces. Students can see on the checklist where they are proficient in their work and where they can improve. The rubrics are formative diagnostic tools to individualize instruction. For example, the sample checklist below shows a student's consistent use of the elements line and shape and principles of movement and emphasis. But it also shows that the elements of value and texture as well as principles of balance, repetition, and contrast require more instruction or review for the individual student. This formative checklist gives you and the students an overall view of their portfolio work as well as the vocabulary for discussing their artwork.

Chart Two
Vocabulary and Checklist for Visual Art

Elements of Art
Line: separation of space
Shape: continuous enclosed line
Value: gradations of light on planes
Color: spectrum within light
Texture: applied or implied tactile planes

Principles of Design
Unity
Balance: radial, symmetrical, or asymmetrical use of elements in a composition.
Movement: direction of elements, top/bottom, left/right, backward/forward in space.
Repetition: duplication of an element that organizes and connects real/imaginary space.
Variety
Dominance: elements that direct the visual movement toward an important focal area.
Emphasis: meaning associated with one or more elements of art (i.e., softness of a line).
Contrast: elements that are opposites create visual interest (warm/cool, light/dark).

Formative Checklist for Art Elements and Design Principles

Portfolio Work	1	2	3	4	5	6	7	8	9	10	Total
Line	X	X		X	X	X	X	X	X	X	9
Shape	X	X	X	X	X	X	X	X	X	X	10
Value			X			X		X			3
Color	X	X	X	X	X		X	X	X	X	9
Texture			X		X	X	X	X			5
Movement	X	X	X	X	X	X	X	X	X	X	10
Repetition	X	X					X		X	X	5
Balance			X				X	X	X	X	5
Dominance	X			X	X	X	X	X	X	X	8
Emphasis				X	X	X	X	X	X	X	7
Contrast					X		X		X	X	4

Students often will need to slow down, making only one or two changes from their previous work, so they understand how those changes affect the direction of the overall portfolio. Sometimes the work just needs more control over a medium or technique. Other times, the meaning of the subject matter needs additional clarity. After a few choices, students will reflect on their work and decide what they will keep and where they will introduce something new. This avoids "jumping around" without reflection or choices that are unrelated. I remind students that there are only two decisions that an artist makes: the idea or subject matter (visible first in the mind of the artist) and the medium of expression that would communicate their idea. The goal of an art curriculum is to teach artistic thinking processes. Suzanne Langer (1955) describes this cognition as "making the invisible, visible…and non-discursive, discursive." Chart Three summarizes the visual arts standards into four categories: creating, presenting, responding, and connecting. The prompts will help you identify where students are already proficient and what they need to focus on moving forward.

Chart Three
Prompts for Visual Arts Standards

STANDARDS CRITERIA	Consistent Evidence	Clear Evidence	Some Evidence	Not Yet Evidence
CREATING	How would the material choices change based on changes in my subject matter?	What other materials would communicate the same subject matter?	What subject matter would these materials communicate?	What classroom materials/ resources are interesting to me?
PRESENTING	How can I share my personal experiences with others?	Which ideas are related to personal experiences?	What ideas can those elements communicate?	Which elements of art are my strengths?
RESPONDING	How can my ideas extend or alter the personal meaning in my work?	Do any of my ideas have personal meaning attached to them?	Which thoughts or ideas do I like or dislike?	Can I recognize my own thoughts and ideas?
CONNECTING	How can I add something novel to the work of others?	How is my work different from the work of others?	How is my work similar the work of others?	Whose work do I admire or emulate?

Some students struggle making choices with subject matter or materials. They insist, "I need an assignment!" In Ceramics, I direct them to a poster for constructing a teapot. Then I just wait for it to happen…and it *always* happens. Within three days, I receive a complaint. "Why do I have to make a teapot when everyone else is doing something different?"

"Do you *know* what you want to make?" I ask.

"Yes!" It may take a few days for students to recognize their own thoughts and ideas. We rarely ask students what *they* are thinking. And ideas go through an incubation process that "occurs preverbally, before logic or linguistics come into play… through emotions, intuitions, images and bodily feelings" according to Root-Bernsteins' (1999) creative thinking model. Patience. They must start somewhere. If you listen long enough, students will edit their own thoughts. Often they will have a solution embedded in their question, such as "Is this color ok, or should it be more of a red-violet?" Or suddenly a student will say they followed "whatever popped in my head." Accept all ideas *except* those potentially harmful to themselves or others such as violence, sexism or racism. Redirect those students towards a subject matter that is related to their idea but extends its personal meaning. Students can fail initially to execute an idea but then succeed with experimentation, called "controlled floundering." The idea cannot be so easy that students become bored or so difficult causing anxiety, but that pleasurable mental state of flow where "Learning for its own sake is rewarding" (Csíkszentmihályi, 1990). This is the intrinsic motivation that causes brain neurons to grow dendrites, making connections between previous learning and new knowledge (Tate, 2003).

Some of my colleagues express frustration when trying to help students verbalize an idea. You can start simply with a question and form the student's answer into another question, called the Socratic method. Robert Genn (2004) suggests web-thinking which is a mind mapping strategy of starting with random ideas and connecting them to other thoughts creating an overall "web" idea. Other methods begin with a definition, a noun, a verb, an adjective given by the student to describe a personal experience. Dweck (2007) in her theory of mindsets, states that the critical ingredient to success and achievement is "evidence of growth." Regardless of the curricular requirements, a growth mindset is only possible when students follow their intrinsic motivation to learn. Teaching students to recognize preferences and trust their own thinking will lead them to original ideas.

One mother frantically came into the art room during parent night asking how to help her child. She had just been conferencing with her son's first grade teacher and was told that his drawing was *behind grade level.* I knew this student to be wildly creative and had no concerns about his ability at age six to draw with accuracy. But the classroom teacher said the student's drawing was evidence of far greater problems. His lack of eye-hand coordination would hinder his ability to *read* and *write.* I am sure it was difficult keeping him on task, sitting at a desk reading or writing! But what he learns in *first* grade is that an extrinsic curricular benchmark supersedes his intrinsic developmental needs.

He compares his drawing with peers from a display on a bulletin board and believes that he cannot draw. Instead of improving his eye-hand coordination, which is important for reading and writing, the classroom teacher inadvertently stops the student's motivation to *continue* drawing which would achieve the curricular goal!

Herein lies the dichotomy. Student motivation is often a comparison between an individual and others in the same class. The resulting comparisons are normative and homogeneous. But not all grading rubrics are the same. For example, the above mentioned first grader received an "A" in art for his insect pin assembled from found materials. The color was dark blue and ominous. And it had a jillion legs and wings. My prompt was "Imagine you discover an insect from another planet. What does it look like?" This is artistic imaginative thinking. When studying insects in their regular classroom, however, the students learned the *correct* parts of insects. At the end of art class students line up at the door with their "space insects" to pin them on my display. A disapproving look from the first-grade teacher eyeing their insect pins sends a powerful message to her students. Their insect pins are incorrect. They did something *wrong*. But the student behavior in the art lesson is entirely appropriate. The "bugged" classroom teacher simply has expectations that are more extrinsic. Many subtle reinforcements of curriculum, occurring every day, shape a child's negative belief in themselves, and their ability to learn.

The Collaborative for Academic, Social, and Emotional Learning seeks to support our schools by advocating "self-efficacy," the belief students have in themselves, their strengths, and abilities (CASEL, 1994). Kristin Hinton explains, "Students who believe in themselves consider problems as challenges to overcome rather than threats to avoid. They will more likely try difficult material until they master the content. They also develop a deeper interest in learning, viewing negative feedback as constructive and quickly recover from setbacks. But students who are not intrinsically motivated avoid challenging tasks out of fear of failure. They believe challenging tasks are beyond their capabilities. They focus on personal shortcomings, give up easily, losing confidence with negative feedback or setbacks." Student self-efficacy develops by exercising their intrinsic motivation to learn. This requires an open curriculum so students can be autonomous, free to move and explore classroom environments, and to recognize their interests in tools, materials and subject matter.

Opening the curriculum is daunting. You may feel a loss of control watching students broaden and stretch *your* interpretation of the curriculum. When students interpret curriculum it comes alive through their own experiences. They move beyond perceived limitations and step over arbitrary criteria searching for a personal connection with their work. You know the students are engaged with curriculum when something happens that comes out of nowhere, out of context and totally unexpected. Those teachable moments with individual students occur more often than we recognize. One of my most challenging and gifted students in Ceramics, for example, produced forty glazes, rather than construct actual clay work. His aesthetic response to glaze-making, not clay forms, determines his curricular goals because the student is initiating independent work, and this is evidence of behavioral growth and change. By the end of the semester, he realizes the glazes need clay pieces to show his work, so we both win. He engages with the curriculum through color and value, then incorporates line, shape, and texture by constructing with clay. When students have the freedom to engage with the curriculum the outcomes are diverse and authentic.

In addition, an open curriculum will help you recognize socio-emotional growth in your students. Though I have taught many students from pre-K age through young adulthood, most of my experience is with teenagers. Not until adolescence can we see how childhood events or generational factors have affected students. Choosing their own subject matter unleashes a virtual tsunami of taboos, family secrets, loss of innocence, and traumas. For example, a remarkable teenager walks into my art room one semester and declares that he is legally emancipated from his mother. Mom struggles with alcoholism, so the student decides to place *himself* into foster care. His artwork reveals the tension that exists in his relationship with his mother. Many pieces appear as yin-yang images, with contrasting values and shapes. Months later, he comes into class with a beaming smile. His mother came to his wrestling match and is getting help with her addiction. This student's courage and motivation to grow as an adolescent, effects change in those around him.

And Tyler, a very talented art student suffering with autism broke all my preconceived ideas about art education. He only briefly maintains eye contact and uses vocalizations that are difficult to understand. But his aesthetic response to painting revealed the artist within. Tyler's painting strokes were measured, deliberate and created balanced compositions. The emotions expressed through his use of color communicated the "joie de vivre" that came from his love of painting. This student without his disability would have been one of my advanced placement kids. But even with his disability, he achieved art honor cords for his Senior art show. Tyler reminds us that "Art is a form of love. Art is the ultimate gift. Art heals life" (Genn, 2010).

CHAPTER TWO

Documenting Choice-Based Learning

Students consistently achieve curricular goals when they direct their own learning. When allowed to exercise intrinsic motivation, they often forget about grades or other extrinsic rewards. You, however, must document their choices and behaviors to determine growth. The terms *choice, strengths, and standards* refer to three different sources of information that can be documented—the student viewpoint, the teacher viewpoint, and the curricular goals. Each provides a different and important perspective that together offer deeper and more meaningful ways to document achievement. This chapter will start with the student's viewpoint, which is choice-based learning. Lessons begin as open-ended didactic conversations with the goal of identifying student preferences for subject matter and medium of expression.

Suzanna explores the art room looking for a material to demonstrate the color wheel. Some second graders are painting while others choose colored pencils or markers. Suzanna chooses colored yarn. She carefully measures and cuts a long length of each color. Next, she wonders where she can hang them. I encourage her to explore the room for ideas. She finds a tree branch in a corner full of still life objects. I demonstrate making a loop knot with her yarns, and she ties them onto the branch in the order of the color wheel.

Suzanna hangs the branch up on a wall cupboard in the art room. But something is missing. Over the next few classes, she works on other ideas and finally comes to me asking for clay. She then proceeds to make several pinch pots that fit in the palm of her hand. She brings them to me, wanting the bowls to hang from the colored yarn. I suggest that she put a hole in the bottom of the bowl shapes to pull the yarn through and knot the ends. After the clay is fired, she paints them the same colors as the yarns, tying the bowls at the end of each string. In describing her piece, she says, "It's a rainbow, and the bowls are 'catching' the rain." This is choice-based learning. Students choose the classroom materials that interest them and produce an outcome to show their interpretation of the curriculum. In this example, the color study by a second grader gives us more than a simple technique with yarn, or her knowledge about the color wheel. Suzanna tells us the meaning she associates with the work, giving us a verbal interpretation. This kind of learning is metacognition, thinking about one's own thinking. When students are making decisions about their work, they are using higher level cognitive skills (Bloom, 1950). Suzanna's work is still the most beautiful rainbow I've ever seen.

Color Study by Second Grader

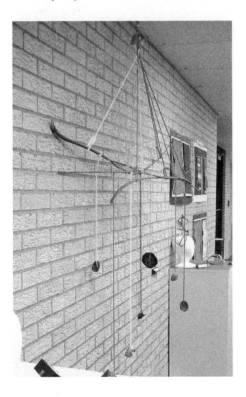 

When viewing curriculum through observation of student choices, the baseline for evaluation is from work the students produce with classroom materials *before* formal instruction. As students begin to recognize and initiate their own ideas, you can begin teaching the curriculum. The assignments and activities you introduce are open to all students who may choose to incorporate them…or not. Students individualize the curriculum by choosing the tools, techniques, materials, and images relevant for their ideas. Evidence for achievement is found in the *relatedness* between the completed works that develop a line of inquiry, an open-ended personal investigation. To be clear, you are still teaching course curricula and all students participate in classroom instruction and demonstrations. The only difference is that you will not grade your assignments or curricular activities. They are informative resources for students as they decide where and in what way they will engage with the curriculum.

Documenting student behaviors from intrinsic motivation is a socio-emotional approach to curriculum. You are now walking alongside your students rather than leading them to one specific curricular objective. I know of no better way to facilitate student decision-making than prompting students using Erikson's stages of development (Erikson, 1954). Socio-emotional growth is as important as cognitive functioning in an open curriculum. For example, a student who has the freedom to move in the classroom exploring materials and resources is exercising autonomy. Their engagement, however, begins when students are motivated to *choose* the art materials for their idea. Next, comes initiative, following through with their ideas to produce an outcome. From here the process repeats itself reaching higher levels of skills and more complex ideas.

Each new piece moves the student inquiry in a direction until the art takes on a life of its own. Students often see what comes next while working on a previous piece. Each development is a surprise as though it came out of the blue. Gradually they begin to understand that the ideas were their own thoughts, albeit on the periphery of their awareness. It's like they are taking a walk inside their heads noticing thoughts and accompanying feelings like budding flowers or falling leaves. Each awareness brings students closer to accepting personal experience as a teacher.

Chart Four are teacher prompts for student engagement and guiding them in choice-based learning. The prompts are in the form of questions that help students use intrinsic motivation to direct their own learning. If you offer suggestions too soon, they will doubt themselves. The time to redirect is later, after students gain confidence in making their own decisions. The far-right column describes student behaviors following extrinsic motivation and thinking. They are the behaviors that trigger dependence and undermine student confidence in their decisions. When you use the prompts, just listen to the students' responses and reflect their own thoughts back to them like a mirror or tape recorder, preferably as questions. The far-left column are the socio-emotional skills documented by Erikson (1950) that nurture continuing growth and development.

Chart Four
Prompts for Student Engagement

Intrinsic Motivation	Teacher Prompts for Student Engagement	Extrinsic Motivation
Autonomy: Explores various resources in the classroom independently.	**Prompts:** *Where are the choices?* *What materials interest you?* *How are you thinking or feeling about it?* *How can you share your ideas?*	**Dependent:** Closely follows teacher directions and assignments.
Initiative: Defers judgment to incorporate mistakes and continues work.	**Prompts:** *What happened?* *Can you incorporate the mistake?* *What will you change next time?* *Where can this idea take you?*	**Perfection:** Perfectionistic fear of making mistakes.
Industry: Recognizes their ideas or interests and plans outcomes.	**Prompts:** *What are you trying to say or do?* *How might you communicate that?* *How successful was that idea?* *What are you good at?*	**Avoidance:** Unable to follow through with plans/ideas.
Identity: Understands how their work is different from the work of others.	**Prompts:** *How do you find your ideas?* *Who inspires you?* *How is your work unique?* *Where do you see yourself in your work?*	**Imitation:** Appropriates ideas from the work of others.
Intimacy: Identifies areas that have personal meaning in their work.	**Prompts:** *Is there a context for your subject matter?* *What context best fits your subject matter?* *Where do you convey feelings?* *Who shares your feelings?*	**Indecision:** Uncertain about personal connection to their work.

Generativity: Recognizes social issues within their own work.	Prompts: *Where is there conflict in your work?* *Do you see any opposing ideas?* *Are they parts of a larger whole?* *Can you explain the paradox?*	Apathy: Indifferent toward social issues or problems.
Integrity: Broadens subject matter to include multiple points of view.	Prompts: *What is your point of view?* *How is that true for you?* *What is true for others?* *Can you create a universal idea?*	Bias: Expresses only one personal point of view through subject matter.

Students gain confidence and control over their materials by repeating the same idea through multiple works. They begin to recognize "mistakes" and learn to defer judgment, continuing to problem solve rather than giving up. No one work is good or bad, just an idea or direction to pursue. Over time, students develop a unique quality, attribute, or technique in their work that communicates personal meaning. They ask for the opinions of others to gauge whether the work is expressing their personal intent. This open dialogue is possible because students see that their work is different from others. Feedback does not represent failure or competition. Rather, critiques help them understand how their overall work has a line of inquiry, underlying questions that connect them with a larger social context. As a result, the scope of their work widens and deepens. Advanced students who continue their portfolio work in this way begin to recognize paradox, seeing opposites as pairs of a greater whole. They also confront personal biases where some of their ideas or beliefs appear to contradict each other. The use of the teacher prompts to engage a student's socio-emotional skills is another way to direct them through the curriculum.

Chart Five is a formative rubric that documents the socio-emotional behaviors of students through choice-based learning. It is a different way of measuring development. The formative rubric documents those "ah-ha" moments when a student's behavior changes to reflect areas of maturation. The scores on the rubric refer to the student work of Olivia in a high school Advanced Studio class. Her work is evidence that socio-emotional skills support curricular goals. Olivia begins her portfolio work choosing markers and watercolors to draw imaginary flowers, working independently. The forms stylize and repeat schemas from memory (1), showing evidence of exploration and engagement with curricular materials. Then she begins working from still life objects such as teacups (2), improving accuracy in her drawing skill. Olivia uses free-form imaginative drawing to balance her compositions. Her work continues with imaginary planes of overlapping shapes in a repeat pattern (3) over several pieces. She then combines an imaginary background as a table surface with observational details of the cup and saucer from an aerial point of view (4). This combination of viewpoints is a recognizable technique that characterizes her work. Realism, without losing her unique point of view and playful imagery, places her within the abstract expressionist movement.

Figure 1

Figure 3

Figure 2

Figure 4

Olivia relates flowers and the teacups with female figures in her family and the strong connection she feels toward them. The objects representing female relationships became collages using advertising images from the 1950s, washer/dryers, telephones, etc. (5, 6, 7). She uses her collage technique to connect with an era her mother and grandmother would have known before she was born. She interprets her work as "holding onto the values of strong women in her family" while adapting to the changing gender roles in society. This reflects intimacy with subject matter through her maternal relationships.

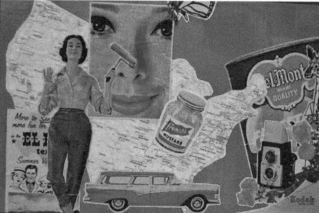

Figure 5   Figure 6

Figure 7

Olivia's choices reflect changes between subject matter and media, use of reference materials and reflections that interpret her work. She follows a line of inquiry creating a body of work that expresses her generational ties. There does not appear to be a viewpoint that addresses social gender issues yet. The work does compare the isolated life of a household woman with increasing social mobility and freedom. But the responsibilities of motherhood and family remain a dominant theme. Prompting for next pieces could address issues for women as they balance family roles and career opportunities in the outside world.

Students can choose the domain criteria and level of proficiency they will accomplish in the following rubric. Then, using the inquiry prompts across the rubric horizontally will help students achieve a higher level of proficiency in a particular area. You can also redirect them down vertically on the rubric to engage with new skills that broaden their learning.

Chart Five
Formative Socio-Emotional Rubric

Socio-Emotional Criteria	Consistent Evidence	Clear Evidence	Some Evidence	Not Yet Evidence	Pts.
Autonomy vs. Dependent **Objective:** Intrinsic Motivation/ Choices	Discusses ideas and/or problems with peers and teacher. *How can you share your ideas?*	Selects materials/ resources and experiments with ideas. *How are you thinking or feeling about it?*	Engages with resources in the classroom independently. *What materials interest you?*	Participates in demonstrations/ instruction with teacher. *Where are the choices?*	4
Initiative vs. Perfection **Objective:** Sense of Direction/ Goals	Reflects on completed work/ initiates areas of improvement. *Where can this idea take you?*	Defers judgment to correct or incorporate "mistakes" in work. *What will you change next time?*	Awareness of problem areas in their work. *Can you incorporate "mistakes"?*	Perfectionistic fear of making mistakes. *What happened?*	4

Industry vs. Avoidance **Objective:** Belief in Strengths/Skills	Produces multiple works that show continued growth. *What are you good at?*	Uses classroom materials to develop ideas or interests. *How successful was that idea?*	Recognizes their own ideas or interests. *How might you communicate that?*	Avoids teacher prompts and/or completion of work. *What are you trying to say or do?*	4
Identity vs. Mimicry **Objective:** Meaning-Making/Connecting	Individual work is recognized by technique, genre, or subject matter. *Where do you see yourself in your work?*	Shows/explains how their work is different from the work of others. *How is your work unique?*	Appropriates ideas from the work of others. *Who inspires you?*	Studies the work of others to influence their choices. *How do you find your ideas?*	4
Intimacy vs. Indecision **Objective:** Sense of Belonging/Responding	Work conveys personal experiences in subject matter. *Who shares your feelings?*	Explains how choices reflect past personal experiences. *Where do you convey feelings?*	Identifies areas of personal meaning in their work. *What context best fits your subject matter?*	Indecision about personal connection to their work. *Is there a context for your subject matter?*	4
Generativity vs. Neutrality **Objective:** Communicates/Inclusivity	Work becomes a form of advocacy to challenge social norms. *Can you explain the paradox?*	Shows/explains a series of works that address social issues. *Are they parts of a larger whole?*	Recognizes social issues within their own work. *Do you see any opposing ideas?*	Neutrality toward social issues or problems. *Where is there conflict in your work?*	2
Integrity vs. Bias **Objective:** Universality/Creating	Work integrates paradox into a novel/nonbinary outcome. *Can you create a universal idea?*	Can explain various resolutions of paradox. *What is true for others?*	Recognizes the contradictions as paradox in their work. *How is that true for you?*	Work depicts contrast or opposing ideas. *What is your point of view?*	1

Documenting choice-based student work is not labored or difficult; it is just a piece of the puzzle that records a student's thinking process at a certain point in time. You cannot review one piece in isolation from a student's previous work. Even preliminary sketches or incomplete work can be documented as those ideas may reemerge later. Socio-emotional growth occurs *between* the pieces. When students actively engage in deconstructing previous work and reconstructing new work, a line of inquiry begins to emerge that directs the portfolio. They are asking questions in response to the art. Inquiry is evidence of development in their work. The changes that occur permit us to track and support individual students.

Not all students achieve the same curricular benchmarks at the same time or through the same medium or subject matter, so every student must document their choices and resulting products. Students record their choices of medium and subject matter on postcards in chronological order as in Chart Six. They draw thumbnail sketches; list reference materials and include an interpretation, if any, of their subject matter. The student documented postcards will help you remember their pieces from each class period. References, whether from imagination, visual materials, text, or the work of other artists, give you some insight into their choices as well. On the back of the cards, you can leave notes or write questions to continue a dialogue with individual students.

Each class has a binder in the art room with scored formative and summative rubrics for each student. As students turn in post cards documenting new work, the binders are updated. The socio-emotional rubric is formative and only diagnostic. But the summative rubrics evaluate growth in the art curriculum and are used for grading purposes. Semester exams include a digital portfolio that students create to record their visual work. This process of documenting student work left me feeling that evaluation had integrity and authenticity for the first time in my thirty-year teaching career.

Chart Six
Choice-Based Student Documentation
Student Post Card

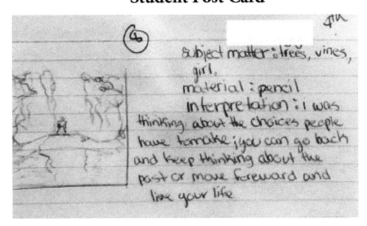

Chart Seven outlines my teaching procedures for choice-based learning. The lesson objectives describe Erikson's socio-emotional stages in seven units of instruction. The seven units correspond with:

- *autonomy* through intrinsic motivation.
- *initiative* for goal setting.
- *industry* to develop skills.
- *identity* through personal connections.
- *intimacy* empathy toward people, places and things.
- *generativity* toward the future.
- *integrity* overcomes bias.

Chart Seven
Procedural Objectives for Choice-Based Learning

Unit 1: Intrinsic Motivation/Choices

1. *Where are the choices?*
   - Explain that you will evaluate curricular goals through student decision-making.
   - Demonstrate how some of the classroom resources connect with curriculum.
   - Review a syllabus which outlines broad areas of the curriculum.

2. *What materials interest you?*
   - Invite students to explore classroom resources.
   - Answer questions students may have about materials.
   - Ask students to collect any resources that interest them.

3. *How are you thinking or feeling about it?*
   - Ask students why they selected certain materials.
   - Discuss how the material relates to an idea they have.
   - Ask students to create a product/problem/experiment about their idea.

4. *How can you share your ideas?*
   - Pair and share product/problem/experiment with a peer or teacher.
   - Study syllabus to find where student work reflects curricular goals.
   - Receive feedback from peers or teachers to confirm work.

Unit 2: Sense of Direction/Goals

1. *What happened?*
   - Identify any problem area(s) of student work.
   - Reflect on how or why that happened.
   - Discuss concerns with a peer or teacher.

2. *Can you incorporate the "mistake"?*
   - Determine if the mistake is major or minor.
   - Try to incorporate the mistake within the work.
   - Follow through with the idea minimizing the mistake.

3. *What will you change next time?*
   - Reflect on what went well in the work.
   - Choose what to keep in the next piece.
   - Allow the next piece to change and evolve.

4. *Where can this idea take me?*
   - Repeat the idea through multiple works.
   - Look for similarities and differences between works.
   - Document previous work and choose a direction to follow.

Unit 3: Belief in Strengths/Skills

1. *What are you trying to say or do?*
   - Ask peers or teachers to interpret student work.
   - Ask students to agree or disagree with feedback.
   - Select interpretations that resonate with students.

2. *How might you communicate that?*
   - Keep the subject matter but change medium/genre/hypothesis.
   - Keep medium/genre/hypothesis but change subject matter.
   - Choose subject matter and medium/genre/hypothesis that agree.

3. *How successful was that idea?*
   - Write down various titles for student works.

- Ask peers or teachers to select the best title for work(s).
- Choose which title communicates original intent.

4. *What are you good at?*
   - Arrange three to five chronological student works.
   - Look for repeated elements between the works.
   - Exhibit works that have relatedness and show growth.

Unit 4: Meaning Making/Connecting

1. *How do you find your ideas?*
   - Research the subject matter of student work.
   - Identify others who have worked with similar ideas.
   - Compare and contrast student work with similar works.

2. *Who inspires you?*
   - Identify the work of those who inspire you.
   - Emulate or incorporate some aspect of their work.
   - Discuss how others can influence student choices.

3. *How is your work unique?*
   - Compare and contrast student work with historical work.
   - Discuss where student work is like the previous work of others.
   - Identify where student work is different and unique.

4. *Where do you see yourself in your work?*
   - Discuss how students identify with their work.
   - Look for specifics in works where students attach meaning.
   - Ask students for an interpretation of their work as a whole.

Unit 5: Sense of Belonging/Responding

1. *Is there a context for subject matter?*
   - Identify subject matter in work.
   - Discuss context as place/background/setting.
   - Describe possible contexts for various subject matter.

2. *What context best fits subject matter?*
   - Discuss how context can change subject matter.
   - Identify possible contexts that extend the meaning of the work.
   - Choose the context that best fits subject matter choices.

3. *Where do you convey feelings?*
   - Find areas in student work where feelings are expressed.
   - Look for an empathetic response with subject matter.
   - Select works to exhibit/present that convey personal feelings.

4. *Who shares your feelings?*
   - Post work on school website and receive feedback from other students.
   - Research organizations/groups that share student interests.
   - Exhibit student work with local organization/groups.

Unit 6: Communicates/Inclusivity

1. *Where is there conflict in your work?*
   - Look for areas of tension or pairing of opposites in student work.
   - Discuss conflict or contradiction between or within works.
   - Pair conflicting works or list areas of contrast.

2. *Do you see any opposing ideas?*
   - Select works to critique and gather one or two peers.
   - Ask students to look for a paradox, opposing viewpoints.
   - Discuss how contrasting works complement each other.

3. *Are they parts of a larger whole?*
   - Select works that could be parts of one larger work.
   - Interpret the meaning of combined works.
   - Ask students how the meaning may be different.

4. *Can you explain the paradox?*
   - Discuss paradox as multiple views that are both true.
   - Demonstrate two views on a similar idea with student works.
   - Ask students to express the paradox in the form of a question.

Unit 7: Universality/Creating

1. *What is your point of view?*
   - Discuss the difference between opinion (like/dislike) vs. point of view.
   - Identify personal point of view in student work.
   - Pair and share students' point of views (beliefs) in their work.

2. *How is that true for you?*
   - Describe where a point of view is expressed in student work.
   - Ask students if their point of view is truthful or honest.
   - Discuss how beliefs may be broader than one point of view.

3. *What is true for others?*
   - Ask students to exhibit one piece that expresses a personal belief.
   - Open the critique to include diverse responses to their beliefs.
   - Use feedback to broaden planning for next product/problem/experiment.

4. *Can you create a universal idea?*
   - Identify parts of previous works that reflect diversity of thought or feeling.
   - Discuss an omniscient (detached) viewpoint that may unite the work.
   - Ask students to combine two different works into one coherent expression.

Having described the process of socio-emotional development the next chapter examines seven choice-based student portfolios. Miles Taylor reworks his childhood memories to achieve a stronger relationship with family, establishing his own *autonomy*. Monica Vicks exhibits the courage to express personal pain, taking the *initiative* to confront bullying at school. Jaden Allen finds *industry* and competence with drawing skill, following his family's hopes and dreams as immigrants to America. Jackie Samonte finds her passion for historic settings and discovers an *identity* with conservationists around the world. Memories of family hunting trips causes Brennen Weil to reflect on the *intimate* connection he has with the natural world. Keydra Celiak *generates* work that challenges social norms and the perceptions of young women through her mixed media collages. Cassie Estro *integrates* restraint and irreverence in a novel image detached from rigid beliefs and binary choices. Each student portfolio demonstrates self-efficacy through open, choice-based outcomes. Their work is proof that qualitative intrinsic motivation is measurable.

I am forever grateful to the many young persons, sharing their work with me and making this book possible. Some of the portfolios include student work spanning several years but most are completed in one year of studio art. Their work documents choice-based learning at the secondary level in south central Wisconsin. In addition, the student works include art courses in Art I, Drawing, Ceramics, Advanced Studio and AP Studio Art. Names are fictitious to protect their identities.

CHAPTER THREE

Choice-Based Student Portfolios

"Growing Independence" by Miles Taylor

The freedom to move and explore the world is autonomy. Our experiences form a kind of "knowing" about the people, places, and things in our surroundings. Learning occurs in the interaction between a student and their classroom environment. The classroom provides the resources and materials for student engagement. As they explore the classroom materials students discover a subject matter or idea that resonates personally for them. In the following portfolio, Miles demonstrates his growing need for autonomy and independence as family relationships emerge in his work.

Miles began in early pieces with mixed media using paint and chalk. Dominant in the composition for piece 1 is the upper left "sun" with an emerging snakelike shape as a focal point. Again, in piece 2, he is experimenting with shapes and lines in tempera paint. The blue fishlike form appears again later in his work.

Then Miles switches to ink and watercolor painting where he chooses female images in his compositions (3). He writes "I'm really inspired by Japanese painting and how much detail in a painting can take only minutes." Consecutive portraits also express strong feelings toward women. Blood drips from their faces (4) because, as Miles writes, "life has been lost…and the blood is hiding her imperfections."

In further work, the faces morph into insects and reptiles (5) using collage materials and techniques. He explains, "This girl is an alien from outer space. She used to be human. But when she was abducted, she lost her senses and her facial features fell off."

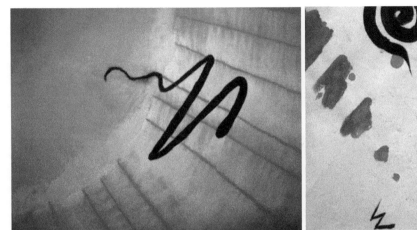

Figure 1

Figure 2

Figure 3

Figure 4

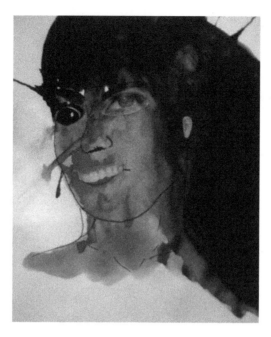

Figure 5

Miles then explores photography and in piece 6 the theme of his portfolio begins to unfold. He depicts an abandoned house with an empty child's chair. In piece 7 the meaning of his imagery becomes easier to visually read in a family portrait. Mom and Dad are simple outlines and three children, Miles and his siblings, are crying black tears. Through this piece, he describes the effects of alcoholism in his family. The image depicts both an absent mother and father. Miles shares that he and his siblings are now living with his grandparents.

In the following image of a whale (8) a change takes place. The dark portraits move to more colorful and soothing images from nature. The painting is a large four-foot watercolor on crumbled and burnt butcher block paper, the figure originating in piece 2. Often students find themselves repeating ideas that have a personal meaning. When Miles and his grandmother came to a teacher conference, I felt the same serenity found in this image.

Next, Miles depicts himself as an infant in piece 9. The self-portrait as a child shows memory of early experiences which he describes as "eating candy and being happy before." In piece 10, a female figure emerges depicting calm, lyrical movement, and an open window to the future. Miles is imaginatively reworking the past, coming to terms with the loss of his parents. The power of his imagination reframes the past in a way that promotes his social and emotional development.

Figure 6

Figure 7

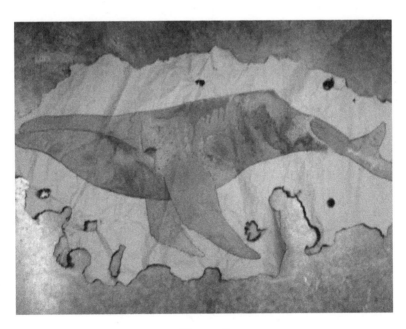

Figure 8

Figure 9

Figure 10

In the student's three-dimensional work, Miles expresses his struggle for independence in a paper mâché self-portrait. He uses magazine text to write on the forehead of a face "sick of your garbage" (11). He then uses recycled materials to vomit the garbage he has taken in from his environment (12). These pieces depict a difficult separation from toxic relationships that interrupt his growth in autonomy. Miles is both accepting and letting go of relationships that are unable to nurture his independence.

In one of his final pieces, Miles depicts a burnt female body in paper mâché (13). In this piece, he builds a mold of a female torso and then torches it to create an image that is decaying. But he attaches nylon filament strings to the inside with golden bones that drop out of the female form (14). He says the bones represent himself, "…the golden child," out of the remains of his mother. Here, Miles integrates past obstacles that are preventing his growth with a confidence in himself to determine his own future.

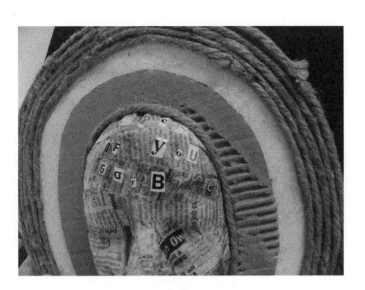

Figure 11

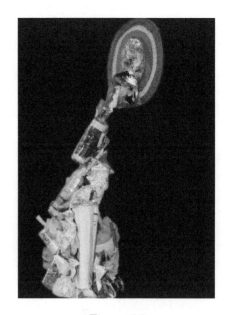

Figure 12

Figure 13

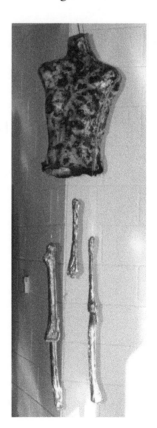

Figure 14

"Developing Initiative" by Monica Vicks

Initiative is the ability to start and continue work through perceived obstacles. Deferring judgment is necessary during this process of choosing information, screening for personal relevance, and producing evidence of growth. This is not easy. Students are making decisions and following lines of inquiry using different materials and techniques. But students can overcome obstacles by trial and error, improving quality and accuracy in their work. Knowing what *not* to do with a piece is equally important. They recognize the limitations inherent in their decisions, whether it is a change in subject matter, technique, or interpretation. Students begin to understand what their ideas can and cannot do. "Mistakes" point them toward the possibilities.

The next portfolio demonstrates the initiative stage in socio-emotional development. Rooted in self-awareness, Monica shows that she can defer judgment to overcome fears of imperfection. She expresses herself through the image of a lone figure who felt "so empty" in piece 1. Piece 2 repeats this figure, but the person is sitting under a tree, in the rain, alone at a gravestone. She cannot move; life is unpredictable and has come to a standstill.

Figure 1

Figure 2

Monica's following portraits distort reality (3) and include an exploding head (4). She writes that her "figures are often cracked and deformed exposing their insides, seemingly in agony because of their distortion."

Monica expresses an interest in the figure, so she joins other students who attend an open figure drawing session at a local college. Piece 5 shows her ability to capture both proportion and feeling tone in the figure. She writes "…you can see the figures becoming less alien and more humanized…They are

Figure 3

Figure 4

Figure 5

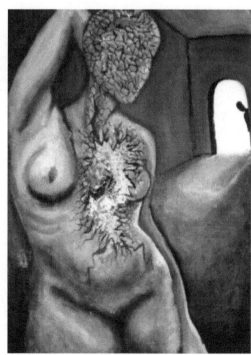

Figure 6

living in a different time and place." In piece 6, she paints a figure with a fire burning in her chest and moving up to her head, like the exploding images previously done in watercolor. In the background is a dark figure. Monica says, "More of her inner parts are being exposed with the cracked glass and exploded guts."

The female form changes again in piece 7, appearing calm and peaceful. Monica uses collage materials depicting earth, water, and sky encircling the figure. She firmly embodies the present where the potential for initiative resides. Monica is keenly aware of the dissonance between self-perceptions and outward appearances. She writes, "These all symbolize the development of me dealing with what I am feeling inside and out."

Figure 7

Piece 8 is a self-portrait in colored pencil representing a softer and more realistic Monica. The subsequent self-portrait in computer graphics (9) depicts herself inside a body during a surgical dissection. Perfection is an idea from outside oneself, often critical and inaccurate. She is battling with the perceptions of others and her own need for acceptance.

Finally, in piece 10, Monica recalls an experience that occurs in childhood. In the computer graphics piece, there are children running and playing freely in the background. But in the foreground is a lonely alien figure. She says, "I always felt different from the other kids, like I was in an alien body." Which all makes sense now. Monica became openly gay in a school environment and society which marginalizes persons who are different, judging them as "aliens." Monica's portfolio work reveals false self-perceptions that her initiative and line of inquiry dispel.

Figure 8

Figure 9

Figure 10

"Accomplishing Goals" by Jaden Allen

Accomplishing goals requires industry, the production of multiple works for students to gain confidence in their skills. Here is where students learn to create variations on previous pieces. During this process, students consider what to keep in their work and what to let go of. Making just one or two changes at a time slows down student decision-making and gives us a visual record of their choices. Over time, relatedness emerges between the pieces. The goal is to develop a portfolio, a grouping of works, which document a student's thinking process from idea formation through production. This process of deconstructing the work involves analyzing previous pieces to construct future work. Students then can put their ideas back together in a new way that creates a change in direction, deepening engagement and extending personal intent.

Jaden begins his portfolio by choosing to draw his tennis shoe in piece 1 using bright colors. Two things are obvious. First, he is working from observation and secondly, he began with something he can draw well, but it is floating in the middle of the picture plane. The tennis shoe is only using one plane of imaginary space, so it appears quite flat. His proportion is accurate, and his color has balance. In piece 2 Jaden repeats the same subject matter but separates the color studies into reds, blues, and whites, adding black.

Figure 1

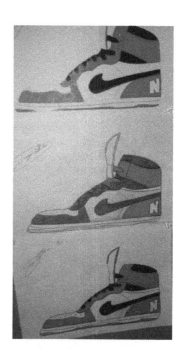

Figure 2

Piece 3 depicts a horse and rider following the idea of movement, but there is overlapping in the figure suggesting a deeper space in the picture plane. The rider's right leg is in an imaginary plane on the opposite side of the horse. The white areas have now become open negative spaces integrating the horse and figure with the background. The next piece (4), shows Jaden's interest in the Beatles when he works from a favorite album, also repeating the tennis shoes. This image continues movement with a horizon line cutting off two edges of the picture plane. Foreground and background overlap and incorporate more depth in the composition, again pulling the white background forward. Movement back and forth in the picture plane indicates growth in spatial awareness.

Figure 3

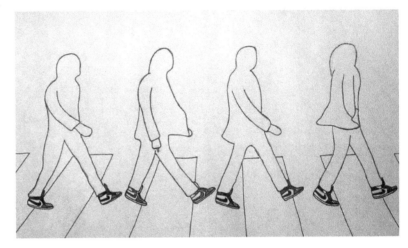

Figure 4

A change in subject matter occurs with a national flag of the Unites States in piece 5. Jaden continues lines of movement in the background as if the flag is waving in the breeze. But some of the colors represent those he associates with Thailand, his immigrant mother's country of origin. This is the first indication of a personal interpretation in Jaden's portfolio work.

Figure 5

Jaden changes his medium to markers, continuing to explore subject matter that expresses the idea of movement. He describes the pieces as "going somewhere." In piece 6 he is shooting into space, exploring the universe, but in piece 7 there is an old car left to rust. Both pieces use a textured method with markers that enhance the idea of motion.

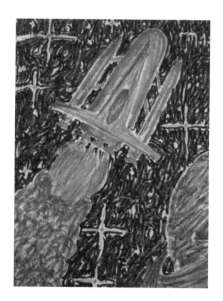

Figure 6

Figure 7

A sailing ship making its way through the ocean, also in markers, pulls us back to the past in piece 8. Piece 9 drops color for sketches in thin line black marker, depicting a woman traveling in a horse and buggy, another older form of transportation. These images from different time periods, are connecting Jaden as a first generation American with the story of his immigrant family. Migration is beginning to emerge as an overarching theme in his work.

Figure 8

Figure 9

Then Jaden begins a series of works about traveling in our contemporary day by automobile. He repeats the use of markers to create value and color in the composition, gaining control over the medium and technique. In pieces 10 and 11, he is experiencing the freedom of exploring the world following highways toward distant horizons, creating more depth in the picture. These pieces also use shapes moving off three edges of the picture plane, which pulls us into the work, making it more accessible to viewers. This ability to mimic perspective is a development in spatial intelligence.

Figure 10

Figure 11

Jaden then imagines all the places in the world he would like to see and collects reference materials to develop his portfolio. Piece 12 shows the detail of the Eiffel Tower in Paris, France, also in markers, and piece 13 is a gondola on the Grand Canal in Venice, Italy, in pen and ink. Again, he continues pulling the viewer farther back into the picture plane. The space is believable as shapes diminish in size toward a focal point.

Figure 12

Figure 13

Figure 14   Figure 15

Jaden continues experimenting with ink in piece 14 but with more natural forms. The boat and water remain, but the textures of reeds and plants are dominant. He changes to pencil in piece 15, which features an old tree, incorporating subtle values and again using overlapping background planes for depth.

As Jaden deconstructs and reconstructs his ideas, something new comes into the work, a range of values from extreme darks to lights. He achieves this by adding charcoal to the ink and pencil pieces previously documented. Images 16 and 17 depict the mixed media technique he used to rework pieces 13 and 15 respectively. The gradations of value create a smoky veil through which Jaden pulled out ethereal lines. He states, "They are like ghosts or mystical figures."

The next piece 18 is a self-portrait alongside a lion. Jaden writes, "My artwork right now is about the naturalistic world and human nature. I realize how we, as humans, construct this messed up world we live in. It could be such a better place. A place where everyone can enjoy it."

Piece 19 is Jaden as an imaginary tribe member, merging lion markings with a self-portrait. Jaden states this synthesis is "connecting me with the distant past, far away in Thailand." Here he brings a personal identification with his mother's immigrant history. Jaden demonstrates full control over lines, shapes, and values to produce an image that is three-dimensional even in shallow space. He accomplishes a broad range of drawing skills with effective manipulation of media. Jaden naturally incorporates all the elements of art and principles of design which are curricular goals. In addition, he depicts with confidence the generational changes within his immigrant family and their dream for him in America.

Figure 16

Figure 17

Figure 18

Figure 19

"Finding Identity" by Jackie Samonte

Student identity forms when their work grafts into the work of others while retaining a personal quality. In other words, ideas belong to everyone, but students will choose ideas that resonate with them. Over time, a unique style or technique emerges that distinguishes their work. For example, the idea of combining different viewpoints in a painting came from Cezanne. Picasso appropriated this technique which led to his style of Cubism. Jackie's work as a watercolorist is identifiable through her treatment of textures in landscapes echoing the work of Ansel Adams and the Sierra Nevada Mountains.

Jackie's interest in nature reflects the subject matter choices in her portfolio. In piece 1 she shows overlapping planes with a fence in the foreground and background and a tree in the middle ground plane. There are some lights and darks, textured leaves, and grass, plus use of line, color, and shape. She is experimenting with space, abstracting from what she knows about real space to create the landscape. Her primary concern is with foreground, middle ground, and background planes where shapes overlap to create the illusion of perspective. In addition, she permits lines to extend off the edges of her paper, suggesting that the landscape continues, beyond those boundaries as a believable space. In piece 2, the student adds a stream and duck in the focal area, moving the tree and fence closer to the top edge of the picture plane. She is experimenting with the viewpoint, now looking down on the landscape, an aerial view. Next, her interest changes to weather effects, choosing a reference of a tornado to fill the sky portion of the landscape (3). The following piece changes seasons from summer to autumn with contrasting warms and cools (4). She is also indicating perspective with the diminishing size of trees toward the horizon line. Each of these innovations are symbolic representations Jackie uses to communicate her ideas.

Figure 1

Figure 2

Figure 3

Figure 4

Jackie began using a grid to help her visually measure space. Over time, a grid is no longer necessary as she can coordinate points, lines, and planes mentally, developing her spatial skills. Below is an example of a grid over a picture (left) as a reference for the drawing (right) of an eye. The horizontal and vertical grid lines provide students with reference points to increase accuracy. Representational drawing skill in many ways is mathematical. Drawing translates visual relationships into a mathematical spatial construct.

Grid Drawing

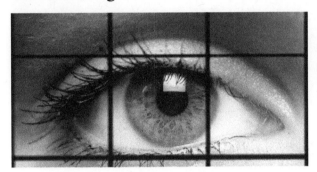 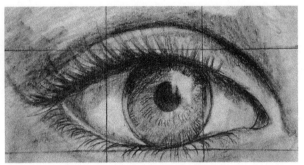

As Jackie considers subject matter, she decides to paint the Grand Canyon. In piece 5 she shows control over the watercolor medium using subtle washes of color and value. The edges of her shapes also begin to define both foreground and background planes in receding horizon lines. All her work now focuses on her references and trying to depict, as accurately as possible, the textures in nature. Over time, she can "sight" measure perspective in creating her work. For piece 6 she chooses an image of Uluru/Ayers Rock. The detail in color, value, and texture of her watercolor technique shows continued refinement. Edges are clearly delineating space according to her viewpoint.

Jackie's love of landscape draws her to continue painting historic conservation sites. Piece 7 depicts the Great Barrier Reef. The horizon line rises and beautiful textures and colors of the reef and ocean merge in this seascape. Again, she uses mathematical perspective to create a sense of space. The coral rocks diminish in size through the middle ground. Her increasing detail in texture and color provides interest in the foreground areas. Jackie's ability to represent perspective continues to develop her drawing and painting skills.

The Mount Everest piece (8a, 8b) shows the economy of technique that begins to identify Jackie's style. Textures lay over subtle washes of color. Values change every several inches recording the play of light on the gigantic snow-capped rocks. The accuracy of her representation conveys a mathematical understanding of form. She is interpreting every point, line, and plane in real space to a painting surface that is imaginary. This level of skill is "visual touch," as though the viewer can feel the texture of the forms that Jackie is representing.

Figure 5   Figure 6

Figure 7

Figure 8a

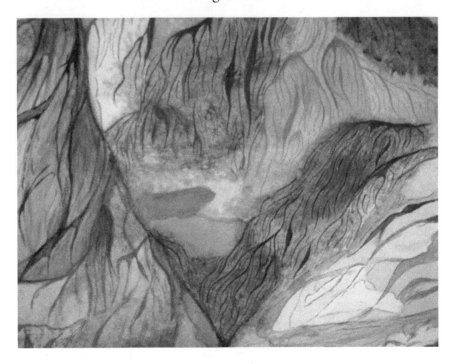

Figure 8b

In piece 9, Jackie is working from observation of a large conch shell and interprets the form as a landscape using the same textural designs over her washes of color and value. It is as though you can crawl right inside the shell. The sequoia (10) puts the viewer at the base of the majestic tree looking upward toward the vanishing point, this time imagining its disappearance in the not-so-distant future.

Figure 9

Figure 10

Jackie's work is identifiable as landscapes, but her painting technique and interpretation of nature distinguishes her work from the work of others. We can recognize her work because the textures are original and unique. Before this journey, Jackie doubts her artistic ability. But following her strengths she discovers an identity with artists around the world, drawing attention to the preservation of beauty in nature.

"Mutual Relationships" by Brennen Weil

Intimacy takes identity to another level. It is possible in any curriculum to achieve a level of mastery, which in spatial skill is representational accuracy. However, artists also communicate a personal connection with their subject matter. This requires planning and producing successive works until a level of intimacy with the subject matter becomes the focus of inquiry. References are jumping off points that combine with other reference materials to interpret meaning from the subject matter. Now, emotional content becomes more important than exact representation. Modification of the curriculum to permit the expression of a personal voice is critical. Without permission and approval from teachers, this level of development is difficult to achieve. Curricular restraints often pull students back into a "grade consciousness" that limits and curtails the choices they make. Intimacy in art is a mutuality with the subject matter, finding one's place in relation to forms in our environment. This is a viewpoint from within the form itself, not as an outside observer. The artist becomes an integral part of the work, revealing the world as they see it.

Brennen starts his portfolio with excellent drawing skills. He works from observation or visual references and relies on them to complete his work. His approach is mathematical, perceiving the relationship between the vertical and horizontal axes of the picture plane. In pieces 1 and 2, Brennen shows his control over pencil, depicting a crane and owl with accuracy and detail. He demonstrates a high degree of spatial awareness in the pieces, integrating line, shape, value, and texture.

Figure 1   Figure 2

Pieces 3 and 4 are experiments with watercolor and ink. The landscapes create a mood of calmness and serenity, more emotional in content, and with more depth in the picture plane. Changing medium from pencils to brushes and washes permits Brennen to become more expressive and freer with technique.

Figure 3

Figure 4

Brennen loves to fish and hunt. He begins to focus on the pheasant and memories of hunting with his father. The close-up portrait of the pheasant feels personal as he changes to colored pencil in piece 5. Again, with watercolor in piece 6, he minimizes line and shape, using color to capture the pose of the subject matter.

Next, Brennen uses watercolor (7) and acrylic (8) to represent the movement of the pheasant flying away. This group of works expresses an identification with nature beyond observation. Rather than depicting the pheasant in a mathematically accurate drawing or painting, he captures the flight and adrenaline rush between the hunter and the bird.

Figure 5

Figure 6

Figure 7

Figure 8

Brennen changes subject matter in piece 9 but continues developing a freer painting style to express the movement of Koi fish. In piece 10 he brings us up close enough to meet the subject face to face.

After studying a variety of natural forms and experimenting with technique and media, he discovers an interest in Indigenous Native (11) culture. He perceives that they are closer to nature. This awareness reflects a shift from studying nature to understanding our relationship as human beings with our environment.

Figure 9

Figure 10

Brennen continues with portraits from other cultures (12) returning to the tighter more detailed use of pencil. He began studying the figure, drawing detailed images of bones (13) and muscles. He states that he has "an interest in human impact on the environment."

The scream (14) is the first portrait that expresses anger or pain, reflecting his frustration with a world so indifferent and removed from nature. Then he found interest in the figure drawing sessions at a local college and his style became freer again, working with charcoal and ink/watercolor washes (15, 16).

Figure 11

Figure 12

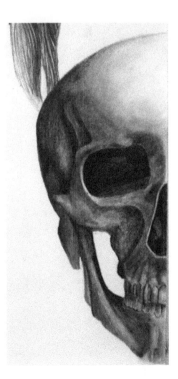

Figure 13

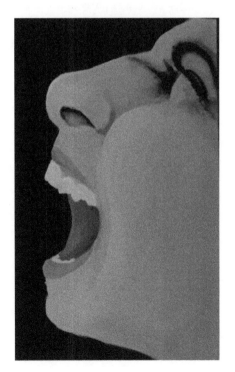

Figure 14

Figure 15

Figure 16

Brennen's portfolio shows development from identification with subject matter, to an awareness that he shares a role in relation to his environment, the context out of which we grow and adapt. He develops organic forms to communicate the movement and nature of subject matter, adding meaning to his accurate representations. His work conveys an intimate connection with nature and poses questions about how we should live in relation to this world.

"Social Contributions" by Keydra Celiak

Generativity is when individuals stand against social norms and attempt to shape society. This has found its way into curriculum through programs to address the moral development of students. In the visual art domain, an artist who stands against a social norm paves the way for others and shapes emerging styles. The following portfolio of student work demonstrates an ability to address social issues from a personal point of view.

Keydra starts painting with acrylics in an impressionistic technique. She works with landscapes (1). Then a skull emerges in the foreground (2) creating a contrast with the peaceful landscape. Her seascape (3) also has high contrast both in values and colors with a sky that is on fire. In piece 4 she changes subject matter to a fierce tiger in watercolor. Then piece 5 depicts the tiger clawing in water with contrasting warm and cool colors.

Figure 1

Figure 2

Figure 3

Figure 4

Figure 5

Keydra continues to paint but her interest moves from animals to portraits (6) and symbolic drawings around her hand (7). This leads to an interest in henna painting (8, 9).

Figure 6

Figure 7

Figure 8

Figure 9

Keydra doodles a lot on notebooks during other classes and brings the drawings with her to art. Piece 10 is about her experience in school in the middle of the week, specifically on Wednesdays. She says "the knife is going through the skull because by the middle of the week, school is mind-numbing." In piece 11 red angular shapes "trap" the figure.

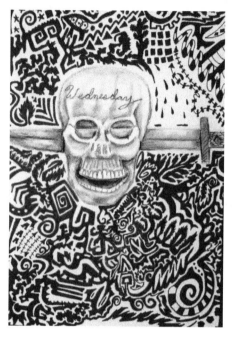

Figure 10

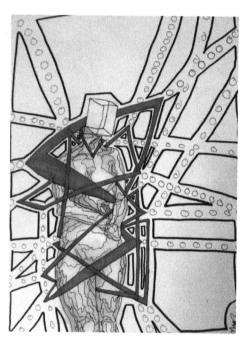

Figure 11

Piece 12 introduces more color but also a sad crying eye with black tears. Then Keydra starts working with collage images from magazines, mostly images about women (13). Here, she cut parts of the face and reorganizes them to bring the magazine image into her imaginative drawing style. She is deconstructing her own perceptions of femininity.

In piece 14 Keydra interprets the "Prom Queen as a garish representation of the female form, painted over and dripping black tears." This prom queen rejects the idea of a beautiful female put on a pedestal for admiration. She expresses feminist values in this piece by questioning cultural views about women. Piece 15 uses a Cover Girl magazine to suggest there is a "field of grenades surrounding our desire to be socially acceptable as women." She portrays a contrasting view of gender identity, challenging conventional thought.

Figure 12

Figure 13

Figure 14

Figure 15

In pieces 16 and 17, Keydra looks closely and critically at an industry that promises beauty and fragrance in exchange for profits, locking women into stereotypes.

In piece 18 Keydra shows the insidious way technology in our society controls a woman's self-perception. Again, the figure is shedding black tears. The primary concern in her work is the freedom of young women to challenge cultural ideas about beauty. Keydra brings an individual voice to the social construct of gender identity. Her work reaches the level of commentary and as such will influence her generation.

Figure 16

Figure 17

Figure 18

"Transcending Viewpoint" by Cassie Estro

Integrity is evident in student art when the work unifies conflicting ideas. The content of the subject matter has verisimilitude or universality, a sense of truthfulness in both personal experience and in the social milieu. In other words, the student incorporates social views and transforms them. Jung describes this experience as the transcendent function, and this philosophy describes my understanding of students who exhibit spiritualist themes in their work (Storr, 1983).

Some may question whether this level of development can occur during adolescence. It is rare. But I have seen student portfolios that explore metaphysical or spiritual questions. It is, for me, the most difficult portfolio to instruct, partly because of the social taboos against spirituality in schools, but also because the individuals carry the proverbial weight of the world on their shoulders. There are bad things that happen for which they have no control yet feel immense responsibility. They may be vegans or join campaigns for social justice issues, the humane treatment of animals or eco-friendly consumerism. They sometimes talk about a significant person who has a strong influence in their lives. The following portfolio asks questions about the nature of life, death, afterlife, and the existence of God.

In the first two pieces, Cassie demonstrates existential awareness, where opposing views—fire and ice—are held together. Piece 1 represents female empowerment. She is holding a flame, symbol of power. Piece 2 is ice, that also represents empowerment, but in this case, it shows that "empowerment can cause someone to grow cold, which means they can get uncaring and bland." In contrast to the female figures Cassie writes about her "concept of the character Sevenson that I have been drawing since I was in 8th grade. I think he definitely represents a part of me because I feel as though he is somewhat of an 'alter-ego' that possesses traits opposite of what I dislike about myself" (3,4). This alter-ego represents an effort to find equilibrium and balance in the student's self-perceptions.

Cassie reworks her memories of childhood as a little girl. She describes piece 5 as "a little girl with a plague mask who is engaging in things that are harmful to herself and others. A plague mask is typically worn to protect someone from the plague, but she is the plague itself." This image expresses two contradictory ideas, the innocence of childhood and the existence of evil. She says it represents "different parts of me at a time when I was considered a destructive person." Here, she is identifying the evil part of herself as her gender. Then in piece 6, the same little girl depicts someone "more tranquil because of the light yellow, excess of white, and feathers. It shows the girl in a veil and holding flowers, so one can assume it refers to the purity of marriage. It also brings some religious elements into it like the upside down cross on the rosary." The painting depicts the opposite of the image in the last piece. She explains "Once again, it represents parts of my own life that were 'cover-ups' of what I did or was feeling." Here Cassie is experiencing conflicting views of her childhood.

Figure 1

Figure 2

Figure 3

Figure 4

Figure 5

Figure 6

In piece 7 Cassie portrays the same little girl, but now older writing "She is wearing a corset to control her body shape. This represents the superficiality of appearance and trying to attain cultural acceptance." She also is scratching a cross into herself, which reflects the religious influences in previous pieces. Cassie continues "I believe it shows the need to do good things but failing because it's done in a bad way. I think after this piece I realize I made her skin black and white so it can seem like a clean slate, like it could be me or anyone." She is identifying with others and the silent suffering that occurs when we do not measure up to cultural norms.

Piece 8 is a portrait of Marilyn Monroe as Cassie describes "I drew this because I was transitioning to a point where I felt like it was time to take my life into my own hands and become more independent." Cassie's choice of Marilyn Monroe reflects a willingness to accept all aspects of her life. Marilyn was a tragic figure, but the student saw her as a person struggling to be herself, free and independent.

About piece 9, Cassie writes, "I needed to take time to just chill out. I also felt like I wanted to get so far but I was just staying in the same place, and I did not know how to get to where I wanted to be."

Figure 7

Figure 8

Figure 9

Figure 10

More imaginary figures dancing freely in piece 10 continue Cassie's search for an honest expression of herself.

Then Cassie produces a piece that brought good and evil together by creating an image in piece 11 of a one-eyed clown petting a lion and smoking a cigar. She describes the piece as "vibrant and carnival-y…clowns are entertaining," yet the clown is also taming a lion. This piece shows an acceptance of who she is as an individual, possessing the honesty and integrity of people much older. As an image, the clown expresses her outward happiness and inward suffering. The cigar may symbolize her rebellion and risk-taking, the potential for destructiveness, including the wildness of the lion. Yet she portrays all these aspects of her life together in one unified and compelling image. I read this image as a modern divinity figure like gods and goddesses in Roman art that had human flaws. She is expressing her belief in both the physical and metaphysical worlds of her experience.

When students like Cassie walk into class, I face my own unresolved questions. Her work is so complex, with layers of conflicting emotions searching for adequate expression. These are the students I worry about the most. They are too young and lack the experience to understand the depth of their awareness. They also know that not all teenagers struggle with such questions about life. Cassie is on a road less traveled, which according to Robert Frost, will make all the difference in the world. I have no doubts.

Figure 11

CHAPTER FOUR

Implementing Strengths-Based Teaching

Ask any student about their favorite class and they say, "I like the teacher!" Chances are they like the class because the teacher *mirrors* their own strengths. This is because we teach using the strengths that we identify in ourselves (Hattie, 2015). In the art classroom, for example, students high in spatial intelligence can exercise those skills in a positive and supportive environment. They have an intrinsic motivation to learn curriculum that corresponds to their perceived strengths. This connection with curriculum creates a sense of belonging, a safe place at school.

As we finish a clay project, second graders ask about the next assignment. I respond, "Drawing!" Some kids are happy, but one student comes up to me with a sad look on her face and whispers in my ear, "I can't draw." My heart drops. Who tells a child they cannot draw? Sadly, children compare themselves with others in school, causing a distortion in their self-perceptions (Marsh & Hau, 2003). These perceptions lower student motivation, confidence, and school performance. Children teach us how they learn through their strengths beginning with their first "No!" as toddlers. If a child scores high on verbal or mathematical skills, they will find many opportunities and resources entering school. If not, curricular modifications are necessary to provide the same opportunities for success.

Teachers monitor and adjust for individual differences every day. We know that exercising strengths increases student mastery, that intrinsic "I can do this!" motivation necessary for continued learning (Vansteenkiste, M. et al., 2004). In areas that are more difficult for students, we can teach them to adapt *using* their strengths. Math can be translated for a spatial student through visualization and acting out a story helps bodily kinesthetic learners retain literary knowledge (Wolfe P., 2001). Endless couplings of multiple intelligences can map an individual's neural pathways, their unique way of learning and being in the world. It is as though each intelligence has its own language, which may be why we consider some students "slow." It takes time to think when you are interpreting information through intelligences that are *not* your strengths.

This chapter will focus on the viewpoint of teachers, mediators between curriculum and students. Your role as a teacher is critical because you must continually balance individual needs with curricular goals. Many of our best practices, in terms of methodology, come from Gardner's multiple intelligences theory which states that every individual has a unique combination of strengths. Just as preferences are a more accurate way of engaging students, an individual's strengths will promote mastery, evidence of higher-level cognition. The following student work demonstrates the vital role you play as a teacher.

Brooke begins her work with sketchbook drawings of small lifeless figures losing blood. Another sketch depicts cuts in the paper dripping with red watercolor paint (1). My first thought… "Are you safe?" No response. "Would you like to see a counselor?" She responds, "No." I prompt her to find other images that might extend or explain the meaning of her work. She agrees and looks through classroom reference materials choosing some pictures of wolves and begins working with pastels (2). The wolf pieces emphasize the collective and protective nature of a wolf pack. She brings friends to the art room, during lunch hour, to see her work. They were her "pack." Brooke's identity, within a circle of friends, mirrors her affinity for the wolves. Self-harm evaporates from her work.

Figure 1

Figure 2

Over time, Brooke recognizes her increasing interest in proportion and drawing skills. She changes subject matter to the elderly, which she considers misunderstood and ignored in society. The portraits of Indigenous people emphasize the wisdom that comes with age (3, 4). She writes, "Every portrait represents, in one way or another, an emotion that I feel now or have felt in the past. They express universal emotions we all share." Her drawing skill becomes photorealistic, etching life experience into the folds and wrinkles of her elderly subjects.

Figure 3

Figure 4

Then Brooke completes a series of expressive drawings that communicate a range of emotions. She is broadening and deepening feelings toward herself and others. Portraits 5 and 6 depict peace and anger, respectively. She writes, "I am trying to portray a feeling of happiness and sense of peace during that time…then I felt like everything is falling apart. On the inside, I was screaming and needed some type of redemption." I can comprehend her work more accurately now as resilience and strength replace her vulnerability.

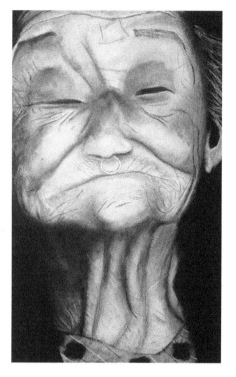

Figure 5

Figure 6

Gardner's multiple intelligences theory challenges educators to recognize and support student mastery in areas of interest and ability. It is difficult, however, to describe how mastery develops within K-12 education or what tools can measure such development. Only students know, for example, if they are hearing music while creating a visual piece, or if a pattern or sequence is present, albeit not obvious in their work. Chart Eight is Brooke's checklist for the six pieces shown above, reflecting her strengths. *All* the works are sensory (visual) because they are images. Piece 1 also depicts bodily kinesthetic (figures) and existential (life/death) intelligences. There is evidence of naturalist (wolves) and existential (contrasting darks/lights) strengths in piece 2. Pieces 3 through 6 show the personal (relationships), bodily kinesthetic (portraits), naturalist (humanity), existential (youth/aging) and spiritualist (wisdom) intelligences. Pieces 4 and 5 also exhibit logical-linguistic strengths because there is mathematical symmetry in the compositions. Brooke's highest scores are existential (6/6) followed by bodily kinesthetic (5/6), naturalist (5/6), and spiritualist (5/6) intelligences. Future work may change those results as she incorporates new ideas, expanding her potential strengths.

The worksheet below, which students complete is an aid to connect their preferences (choices of subject matter and medium of expression) to the intelligences that are probable strengths. The definitions below are how I describe the multiple intelligences when working with students:

Chart Eight
Vocabulary and Checklist for Individual Strengths

Personal intelligences…Dialogue between the individual (self-awareness) and interpersonal environment (people, places and things).

Bodily kinesthetic intelligence…Tactile quality (sense of touch) or physical movement.

Sensory intelligences…Visual images, auditory sounds and rhythms, and culinary smells and tastes.

Logical-linguistic intelligences…Numbers, sequences or chronology, letters, symbols and words.

Naturalist intelligence…Natural forms and environments.

Existentialist intelligence…Social dichotomy/paradox (i.e. good/evil, light/dark, love/hate, male/female).

Spiritualist intelligence…Beliefs about life, afterlife and awareness of physical and metaphysical realities.

Formative Checklist for Individual Strengths

Portfolio Works	1	2	3	4	5	6	7	8	9	10	Total
Personal Intelligences			X	X	X	X					4/6
Bodily Kinesthetic Intelligence	X		X	X	X	X					5/6
Sensory Intelligences	X	X	X	X	X	X					6/6
Logical-Linguistic Intelligences				X	X						2/6
Naturalist Intelligence		X	X	X	X	X					5/6
Existential Intelligence	X	X	X	X	X	X					6/6
Spiritualist Intelligence			X	X	X	X					4/6

Through this tool students are given a better understanding of their choices and *perceived* strengths based on Gardner's multiple intelligences model. Sometimes students identify strengths based on the perceptions of others rather than self-perceptions. Over time, they can recognize and modify those views. The formative rubric, Chart Nine, is helpful when you are measuring both areas of strengths and needs in student work. I combined intrapersonal and interpersonal intelligences as the *personal intelligences* that reflect not only relationships, but the interface between an individual and their environment. This dialogue between the personal intelligences is critical for metacognition, a student's ability to reflect on their own thinking and construct meaning. *Bodily kinesthetic intelligence* is tactile movement in space and time. Spatial and musical intelligences also combine as *sensory intelligences* and include olfactory and gustatory. *Logical-linguistic intelligences* join as abstractions of sensory experience that communicate meaning through symbols. Awareness of paradox indicates *existentialist intelligence*, with contrasting elements or viewpoints. The addition of the *spiritualist intelligence* is adapted from the research of Zohar and Marshall (2006), since I find evidence of similar subject matter in student work, such as religious beliefs or life after death. The rubric depicts scores from Brooke's portfolio work above with drawing materials and portraiture.

Brooke is just beginning to tap into her enormous potential. Her scores indicate strengths in the personal, bodily kinesthetic, sensory, naturalist, and existential intelligences. Areas for growth include the logical-linguistic and spiritualist intelligences. Brook's ability to respond to the materials and ideas in her art builds confidence that she can communicate something meaningful to others. She describes her thinking process and reflects on her work verbally and in writing. Each piece describes a context that shows empathy for natural life cycles. However, only the final piece, the screaming man, begins to move in a direction that is spiritualist, a depiction of anger against mortality. Brooke's formative scores help me direct her instruction, with no assignments but those she gives herself.

Chart Nine
Formative Strengths-Based Rubric

Strengths-Based Criteria	Level 4 Consistent Evidence	Level 3 Clear Evidence	Level 2 Baseline Evidence	Level 1 Not Yet Evidence	Pts.
Personal Intelligences **Method:** Elicit intrinsic motivation of students through preferences for resource materials.	Conveys their idea to classroom teacher/ peers. *How can I share my ideas?*	Recognizes an idea that connects with a personal interest. *How am I thinking or feeling about it?*	Selects classroom resources for their work based on preferences. *What materials interest me?*	Explores materials and resources independently in the classroom. *Where are the choices?*	4
Bodily Kinesthetic Intelligence **Method:** Document student preferences to determine individual goals.	Refines ideas throughout multiple works. *Where can this idea take me?*	Reflects on areas of improvement for their work. *What will I change next time?*	Defers judgment to follow through with an idea. *Can I incorporate the mistake?*	Perceives "mistakes" in their work. *What happened?*	4
Sensory Intelligences **Method:** Direct students toward skills that show competence.	Develops related works that follow a line of inquiry. *What am I good at?*	Produces work that communicates ideas to others. *How successful was that idea?*	Chooses ideas and gathers resource materials. *How might I communicate that?*	Hesitant to follow through with ideas. *What am I trying to say or do?*	4
Logical-Linguistic Intelligences **Method:** Summarize student interpretations of their work.	Interprets personal meaning in their work. *Where do I see myself in my work?*	Identifies the differences between their work and others. *How is my work unique?*	Emulates ideas from the related works of others. *Who inspires me?*	Analyzes the work of others to inform ideas. *How do I find my ideas?*	4

Naturalist Intelligence **Method:** Connect student experiences with broader contexts.	Communicates an affinity for shared experiences. *Who shares my feelings?*	Empathetic response to context and past personal experiences. *Where do I convey feelings?*	Integrates subject matter with context in continuing work. *What context best fits my subject matter?*	Applies place/ background to give subject matter context. *Is there a context for subject matter?*	4
Existential Intelligence **Method:** Critique ideas in student work that appear to be in opposition.	Conveys solidarity with individuals over social norms. *Can I explain the paradox?*	Identifies a personal connection with social justice issues. *Are they parts of a larger whole?*	Interprets contrast as tension between self and society. *Do I see any opposing ideas?*	Demonstrates contrast or dichotomy in work. *Where is there conflict in my work?*	4
Spiritualist Intelligence **Method:** Explore point of view that unites personal and social experiences.	Omniscient viewpoint connects personal/ social experience to create novelty. *Can I create a universal idea?*	Multiple points of view reflect communal experiences. *What is true for others?*	Broadens subject matter to explain viewpoint. *How is that true for me?*	Expresses personal point of view in subject matter. *What is my point of view?*	3
				TOTAL POINTS	27

As the structure for observing student strengths, the multiple intelligences theory reminds me of a field, quite literally. The rows of sprouts wind up and down gentle slopes around trees and rocks and houses that put a claim to it. This field is rich in minerals but not in a uniform way. As a result, certain crops would grow better in different areas of the field. So too, as we learn to recognize the intelligences in student work, we can better individualize instruction. Chart Ten lists student strengths by levels of difficulty from the above rubric. I post the list in my classroom because students can identify exactly where they find themselves on the various levels of achievement.

Chart Ten
Levels of Difficulty for Individual Strengths

Level One
- Explores resources in their classroom independently.
- Perceives "mistakes" in their work.
- Hesitant to follow through with ideas.
- Analyzes the work of others to inform ideas.
- Applies place/background to give subject matter context.
- Demonstrates contrast or dichotomy in work.
- Expresses personal point of view in subject matter.

Level Two
- Selects classroom resources for their work based on preferences.
- Defers judgment to follow through with an idea.
- Chooses ideas and gathers resource materials.
- Emulates ideas from the related works of others.
- Integrates subject matter with context in continuing work.
- Interprets contrast as tension between self and the society.
- Broadens subject matter to explain viewpoint.

Level Three
- Recognizes an idea that connects with a personal interest.
- Reflects on areas of improvement for their work.
- Produces work that communicates ideas to others.
- Identifies the differences between their work and others.
- Empathetic response to context and past personal experiences.
- Identifies a personal connection with social justice issues.
- Multiple points of view reflect communal experiences.

Level Four
- Conveys their idea to classroom teacher/peers.
- Refines ideas throughout multiple works.
- Develops related works that follow a line of inquiry.
- Interprets personal meaning in their work.

- Communicates an affinity for shared experiences.
- Conveys solidarity with individuals over social norms.
- Omniscient viewpoint connects personal/social experience to create novelty.

Some students will look at the above chart and decide to follow all the Level One standards before moving on to higher levels. Those behaviors correspond with the far-right vertical column on the rubric in Chart Nine. They are exploring the wide range of intelligences to find their strengths. They may continue to Level Two which corresponds to the behaviors in the middle right column, and so on. Others may follow Levels One through Four in a horizontal row because they recognize an area of strength and are motivated to reach mastery. Their trajectory might follow as below continuing Chart Ten:

Personal Intelligences
- Explores resources in their classroom independently.
- Selects classroom resources for their work based on preferences.
- Recognizes an idea that connects with a personal interest.
- Conveys their idea to classroom teacher/peers.

Bodily Kinesthetic Intelligence
- Perceives "mistakes" in their work.
- Defers judgment to follow through with an idea.
- Reflects on areas of improvement for their work.
- Refines ideas throughout multiple works.

Sensory Intelligences
- Hesitant to follow through with ideas.
- Chooses ideas and gathers resource materials.
- Produces work that communicates ideas to others.
- Develops related works that follow a line of inquiry.

Logical-Linguistic Intelligences
- Interprets personal meaning in their work.
- Analyzes the work of others to inform ideas.
- Emulates ideas from the related works of others.
- Identifies the differences between their work and others.

Naturalist Intelligence
- Applies place/background to give subject matter context.
- Integrates subject matter with context in continuing work.
- Empathetic response to context and past personal experiences.
- Communicates an affinity for shared experiences.

Existential Intelligence
- Demonstrates contrast or dichotomy in work.
- Interprets contrast as tension between self and the society.
- Identifies a personal connection with social justice issues.
- Conveys solidarity with individuals over social norms.

Spiritualist Intelligence
- Expresses personal point of view in subject matter.
- Broadens subject matter to explain viewpoint.
- Multiple points of view reflect communal experiences.
- Omniscient viewpoint connects personal/social experience to create novelty.

While we can assume that all the intelligences are present at birth, conditions for mastery and individual outcomes are diverse. Not all environments elicit the strengths of every child. Following a whole group demonstration of watercolor painting, for example, some students may continue working as a small group with that medium. Their choices might involve in-depth experimentation, analyzing qualities inherent in the medium, subject matter, or genre. Others may observe instruction or modeling and then return to their current work without showing much interest at that time. Inevitably, a student will ask questions about a previous lesson weeks later. Like planting seeds, ideas need time to root. This is the beauty of strengths-based teaching. You will see evidence of growth in many different directions in your classes. If you become disoriented, it is because you are teaching curriculum from multiple viewpoints. You are learning to teach what you know through *knowing* your students.

One of the properties of learning models is that stages of growth are invariant, meaning that each stage is dependent on the success of previous stages. This does not mean, however, that growth becomes stagnant, or individual strengths are unalterable; rather our way of measuring growth in intelligences must be as fluid as learning itself. Over time, exercising intelligences that are strengths will give students confidence to explore other intelligences. The intrinsic motivation to develop those strengths increases self-efficacy, a sense of confidence, competence, and continued growth. This confidence will translate into less proficient areas and evolve into new interests.

The key to strengths-based teaching is to recognize the individual experiences in student work. Some are reworking memories from childhood. Others are navigating difficult relationships, the on-set of a genetic illness or a significant loss. Cyber-bullying and other traumas also effect the mental health of students. The childhood cloak of innocence no longer protects them. At the same time, we increase their dependence on technology, removing teachers and often parents as primary sources of information and social connection. But *every day* there is a teacher connecting with every student in our schools. We know "the importance of teacher-student relationships cannot be minimized" (John Hattie, 2008).

In 1972 a small rural public school district was in one of the lowest achieving counties in the State of Ohio. Curriculum offered no Advanced Placement classes and the tax dollars per student could not compete with urban and suburban schools. But what do I remember? Mrs. Kortokrax, who brought me historical novels every few weeks one summer. And Mrs. Clark, who put her hand on my shoulder whispering, "Don't stop drawing." It is no surprise that ninety percent of adults remember the specific teachers that taught them self-efficacy, a belief in their own abilities (Brown, 2017).

Our schools are a major catalyst for supporting each student's belief in their ability to achieve. We know that preferences of the student are a determinant in authentic learning (Benware and Deci, 1984). When a student learns how to connect their interests within a domain, they can gain proficiency and even mastery. Gardner further posits that students perform better in other subject areas *after* they engage with their own unique way of learning (Gardner, 1993). My experience tells me that each student's individual strengths, based on their own self-reporting, is a more accurate baseline for instruction and evaluation than standardized tests, grade point averages, or even IQ scores.

CHAPTER FIVE

Evaluating Standards-Based Curriculum

Bloom's Taxonomy remains, with adaptations, the basis of curriculum development since the 1950s. The model is cognitive-behavioral and evaluates students by their ability to demonstrate what they know and can do. The model begins with knowledge level information given by teachers. Students then demonstrate their comprehension by reiterating the information, verbally or in writing. Application of the information takes the form of assignments or testing, usually as written exams. This practice utilizes the first three levels of cognition (remembering, understanding, and applying) but teachers must cover a vast amount of knowledge in every curriculum. Time constrictions create and perpetuate this limited cycle of disseminating information, checking for understanding and evaluating students that repeats itself over and over.

Higher levels of cognition, (analyzing-synthesizing, evaluation and creating), involve students making choices which are informed and influenced by the different experiences each student brings to the curriculum. Students must deconstruct and reconstruct those experiences to create meaning. Open-ended questions or problems give students the opportunity to choose how they will demonstrate *what* they know and can do. This is where the national standards come into play.

Standards align with curriculum to recognize outcomes that are diverse and broaden opportunities for achievement. Art education, for example, has four domains, studio art, aesthetics, art criticism, and the history of art. Students can achieve proficiency in any combination of those areas in an open curriculum. Some will do so by exploring each branch of study. Others will develop mastery in one or two areas following their strengths. They may or may not follow a chronological course syllabus. Nothing about this process or the resulting products is "standardized." This chapter will explore the viewpoint from curriculum and national standards and how they can be achieved in a choice-based art classroom.

Standards in a choice-based classroom provide students the freedom to use their own thinking processes to achieve curricular goals. In this way, they are learning to recognize how they think and problem-solve. For example, I set out some seashells and asked elementary students to draw from observation with as much detail as possible. Following best practices, I demonstrate blind contour drawing and tell students to take a shell and draw at their seats. One second grader, however, leaves her seat to look at a shell more closely and returns to draw what she could remember. Encouraging her to take the shell to her seat, she responds, "No, I have to see it in my head first." That is when I realized that no matter how closely you observe an object or an algebra problem, a *mental* schema is recording those details. These correlations, between real space and the imagination, define spatial intelligence, the strength in an art curriculum.

Students strong in spatial intelligence immediately engage with the materials in art class. They are not hesitant to ask questions, and many do not wait for instruction. They explore and experiment independently. One choice leads to another and yet another, revealing a thinking process, a line of inquiry, unique to each student. Sheldon prefers mostly pencil, as you will see, throughout his work. His subject matter begins with some observational drawing, the crayon box (1) but imaginative memory schemas frequently dominate his compositions. In piece 2 he points us to an enclosed corner of a room with a lonely guitar against a wall and an open door. While many students would explore various materials before choosing a subject matter, Sheldon has a mental picture of his images before picking up his pencil. He writes, "My work is about different views of memory. I take memories and draw them in a way that tells a story. I almost never use color because I do not remember in color, just images of black and white, a million stories a second."

Figure 1

Figure 2

In piece 3 Sheldon places us sitting at a desk in school, measuring with a ruler and then again, holding a gavel as a judge (4). Sheldon writes, "Most are stories with moral ideology or philosophical concepts. One of my favorite ways to convey these messages is through hands frozen in time scenarios, like the judge holding a gavel in a clenched fist and a guilty verdict paper in the other hand. This represents choice and penance."

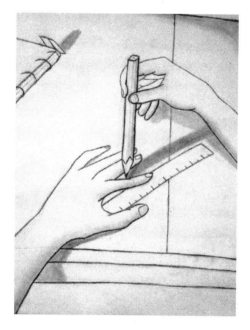

Figure 3

Figure 4

Here is where I begin to document the visual arts standards for Sheldon using the standards rubric in Chart Eleven. He is demonstrating some evidence in three of the visual art domains. He responds to the classroom materials, choosing the pencil medium (aesthetics). He uses observational/imaginative drawing techniques to explore elements of art, particularly line and shape, but also beginning use of value with shadows (studio art). In addition, he can communicate verbally and in writing about his work (art criticism).

Sheldon has yet to explore, however, the past work of other artists with whom he shares ideas. This is when I prompt him to study some art books. Piece 5 is Sheldon's copy of Giorgio de Chirico's *Mystery and Melancholy of a Street, 1914* that resonates with him. This choice places his work with Metaphysical Art, a dreamlike realism depicting the inner mind. The influence of de Chirico's paintings can be seen in Sheldon's continuing work with deeper shadows and more contrast. Here is where

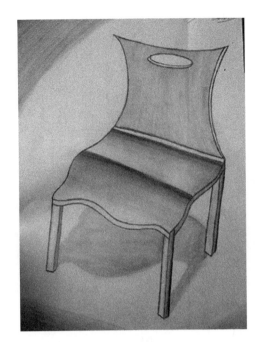

Figure 5   Figure 6

I can document the influence of another artist on his work (history of art) and interpreting meaning that relates to personal experiences (aesthetics).

Sheldon continues to refine his drawing skill with value rendering of a classroom chair (6) and a broken table (7), leading to a broken cross (8). He explains, "Most of the time I try to tell a moral, but sometimes I show the moments when time just stops, when you think about everything that's happened to you and time doesn't seem to exist…moments that everyone forgets." The early crayons and guitar with an exit door represent memories that are gone. The ruler and gavel depict ways of judging the world. The chair and cross that split apart emphasize the binary choices of right versus wrong and Sheldon's breaking away from those rigid beliefs. Those pieces bring his work into a social context with separation and alienation themes.

Piece 9 has a focal point on an empty chair in the middle of a sun-filled room with papers falling out of a drawer and empty bookshelves and bins. No one is there. But a figure emerges in piece 10, an influence from de Chirico. The shadow figure is pointing in a direction as though it is trying to find an exit. The next piece (11) brings us into the picture plane, viewing the way out of a hall with columns. There appears to be a terrain or water to cross leading to stairs and an exit from the space. Finally, in piece 12 Sheldon brings us outside, viewing the house from a distance behind a large tree pushing off three edges of the picture plane. Curious birds are hovering around a scarecrow. Leaves fly as the

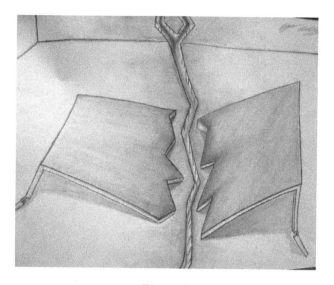

Figure 7

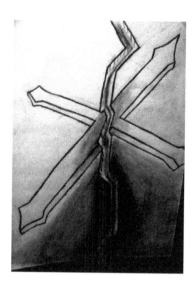

Figure 8

wind blows, changing the seasons. The horizon line is tilted but a pathway remains back to the house. Sheldon explains, "My images are broadening, using more space to explain a story or idea with more objects in the background or shadows of gray and black. My art is conceptual and uses strong values to tell a story hidden in the picture...I never retell a story." He doesn't have to; the images have recorded them. Sheldon's portfolio portrays his growing awareness of a larger world view more immediate than past experiences.

Figure 9

Figure 10

 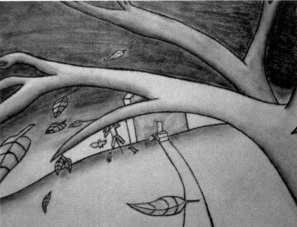

Figure 11   Figure 12

Chart Eleven is a rubric for a standards-based curriculum in art education. It includes the four domain areas in visual art. This opens the art curriculum to students who may have strengths in spatial intelligence but not necessarily studio art. The rubric provides options for students to be successful using preferences, the thought processes unique to each person. Students choose whether they will demonstrate "proficient," "accomplished," or "advanced" scores within the rubric. Sheldon receives credit for his work, even though he does not excel in all the standards. Nor did he experiment with the wide variety of materials available to him. As an instruction tool, the rubric shows us areas where students can grow as well as their accomplishments. In a class where all students are given the same assignment, many would not engage with their strengths as Sheldon did. Some students may not discover their strengths in a curricular area. The rubric opens the art curriculum, reaching students who are artists, philosophers, critics, historians, and any combinations thereof.

Sheldon's portfolio scores are shown for the anchor objectives within each art domain. His advanced scores are in aesthetics and art criticism which indicates two areas of strengths. Predominantly black and white images communicate an austere and distant feeling tone. Yet his writings express a range of very personal emotions. He also scores "accomplished" in studio art, evidence of increasing skill in drawing. In the history of art, Sheldon scores "proficient" as he demonstrates a connection with the art of Giorgio de Chirico. But his work does not add novelty to Metaphysical Art or create a bridge toward Surrealism. This is a strong area, however, for growth.

Chart Eleven
Summative Rubric for National Standards in Visual Art

STANDARDS CRITERIA	Advanced Evidence	Accomplished Evidence	Proficient Evidence	Some Evidence	Pts.
STUDIO ART **Point to Line to Plane** National Core Arts Standards: **Creating** *Procedural Reasoning*	Student can refine ideas by changing materials and/or subject matter. *What can I change to broaden my ideas? (anchor Cr3)*	Student can develop mastery over one or more materials or techniques. *How many ways can I express my ideas? (anchor Cr2)*	Student can organize materials based on subject matter preferences. *What subject matter relates to these materials? (anchor Cr2)*	Student can generate ideas from exploring classroom resources and materials. *What materials are interesting to me? (anchor Cr1)*	3
ART CRITICISM **Less is More** National Core Arts Standards: **Presenting** *Factual Reasoning*	Student can convey a line of inquiry through a presentation of related works. *Can I arrange my work in a sequence or chronology? (anchor Pr6)*	Student can develop a portfolio of work that shows unity and variety. *Which related pieces tell a story? (anchor Pr5)*	Student can interpret meaning and relatedness between their works of art. *Which pieces are related in some way? (anchor Pr4)*	Student can analyze the elements of art and principles of design in their work. *Where are my strengths? (anchor Pr4)*	4
AESTHETICS **The Medium is the Message** National Core Arts Standards: **Responding** *Conceptual Reasoning*	Student can apply ideas to social contexts that will extend their meaning. *How does context change the meaning of my ideas? (anchor Re9)*	Student can interpret meaning from materials that relate to personal experience. *What ideas can these materials represent? (anchor Re8)*	Student can analyze qualities in classroom materials and resources. *What do I like/ dislike? (anchor Re7)*	Student can express their thoughts and feelings in response to a classroom environment. *Do I recognize my own thoughts and feelings? (anchor Re7)*	4

| HISTORY OF ART **Form follows Function**

National Core Arts Standards: **Connecting**

Metacognitive Reasoning | Student can contribute novelty to the work of social, cultural, or historical art.

How is my work unique compared to the work of other artists? (anchor Cn11) | Students can graft their ideas into social, cultural, or historical art.

Where can my ideas complement the work of other artists? (anchor Cn11) | Student can synthesize their work with the work of another artist(s).

How can other artists influence my work? (anchor Cn10) | Student can relate their own portfolio work with the work of recognized artists.

Where does my work fit with previous artists? (anchor Cn10) | 2 |
|---|---|---|---|---|---|
| | | | **TOTAL POINTS** | | 13 |

Grading scores, A 13-16, B 9-12, C 5-8, Insufficient evidence 1-4

The anchor standards in the above rubric show *Creating* (Cr 1-3), *Presenting* (Pr 4-6), *Responding* (Re 7-9) and *Connecting* (Cn 10-11). Creating is the production of studio art. Presenting is exhibiting the work for art criticism. Responding is an aesthetic preference for the subject matter, medium, elements or principles in a work of art. And connecting is placing an artwork into its historical context. Krathwohl's Depth of Knowledge (2002) model corresponds with the four domains in visual art. Factual reasoning is observation of the elements of art and principles of design representing art criticism. Conceptual reasoning is an aesthetic response to ideas and materials. Procedural reasoning is the process of creating art using materials that express ideas. Metacognitive reasoning attributes value to student art work as it may relate to established historical works. Chart Twelve lists the standards and curricular objectives, by level of difficulty, with essential questions using terms from the 5E constructivist model (Bybee, 2015) without the final evaluation stage to avoid "grade consciousness" that may affect student decision-making. Exploration also *precedes* student engagement because students explore before engaging with subject matter or materials in an open curriculum.

Chart Twelve
Procedural Objectives for Visual Art Standards

Level One

Essential Question: What materials are interesting to me? (anchor Cr1)

1. **Student can generate ideas from exploring classroom resources and materials.**
    *   Explore basic art materials on tables or near their seats (paper, pencils, erasers, markers, scissors, glue, tape, colored pencils).
    *   Engage students to imagine a product (problem/essay/experiment) using one or more of the materials, then sketch or construct their ideas with a sheet of paper.
    *   Elaborate by documenting their piece on postcards with a thumbnail sketch, citing subject matter, materials, and an interpretation of why/how they imagined their idea.
    *   Explain that students can explore other classroom resources/materials, including image files and media examples, and continue to document their ideas.

Essential Question: Where are my strengths? (anchor Pr4)

2. **Student can analyze the elements of art and principles of design in their work.**
    *   Explore classroom exemplars on the elements of art and principles of design.
    *   Engage students to study their work and identify clear evidence of any art elements.
    *   Elaborate with a partner and discuss art elements that are not present in the student work.
    *   Explain how the placement of elements describes the principles of design in their work.

Essential Question: Do I recognize my own thoughts and feelings? (anchor Re7)

3. **Student can express their thoughts/feelings in response to a classroom environment.**
    *   Explore thoughts/feelings by asking students to close their eyes and imagine an object such as a chair. Give wait time, then ask them to see as much detail as possible, such as the materials it is composed of, colors, textures, what kind of chair, etc.
    *   Engage students to open their eyes and describe what kind of chair they imagined. Discuss how we can all imagine the same idea, but the significant details are different.
    *   Elaborate on how we recognize, through memory and imagination, our conscious thoughts and feelings that give us ideas. Ideas are visualized before they are realized.
    *   Explain that ideas belong to everyone, connecting similar collective experiences. But what everyone does with those ideas is diverse and unique.

Essential Question: Where does my work fit with previous artists? (anchor Cn10)

4. **Student can relate their own portfolio work with the work of recognized artists.**
   - Explore how other artists influence each other, such as the Post-Impressionist Cezanne and Picasso's study of his works that led to the invention of Cubism.
   - Engage students making a list of nouns and adjectives they would use to describe their work in progress or overall.
   - Elaborate using computer or art history books to research other artists whose work is like the list of nouns and adjectives describing the student work.
   - Explain how they could follow the work of several artists with whom they have an interest in emulating or studying.

Level Two

Essential Question: What subject matter relates to these materials? (anchor Cr2)

1. **Student can organize materials based on subject matter preferences.**
   - Explore various materials and techniques through demonstrations, increasing student options for choice-based work.
   - Engage students through modeling, whether they will choose the materials/techniques or not. Ideas often occur later, so participation is required.
   - Elaborate on the quality of a material that correlates with their subject matter, such as painting captures patterns of light and color in portraiture, or the malleability of clay to form pottery.
   - Explain that if students are between portfolio pieces, they should be working with materials from the demonstrations until they are ready to start a new piece.

Essential Question: Which pieces are related in some way? (anchor Pr4)

2. **Student can interpret meaning and relatedness between their portfolio works.**
   - Explore repeated subject matter using postcard documentation for their portfolio work.
   - Engage a partner and ask them to find some relatedness within each portfolio.
   - Elaborate questions to clarify any meaning or theme documented on the postcards.
   - Explain how feedback from a peer can clarify meaning and interpretation of student work.

Essential Question: What do I like/dislike? (anchor Re7)

3. **Student can analyze qualities in classroom resources and materials.**
   - Explore the idea of preferences making a list of favorites, foods, clothes, etc.
   - Engage one of the student preferences and make an argument to win votes that agree or disagree.

- Elaborate on the underlying values for preferences such as comfort, familiarity, etc.
- Explain why students have preferences for certain classroom materials based on similar qualities inherent or associated with the materials.

Essential Question: How can my work show influence from other artists? (anchor Cn10)

4. **Student can synthesize their work with the work of other artists.**
   - Explore new subject matter or techniques by copying a recognized artist.
   - Engage students to synthesize some aspect of the artist's work into one of their own pieces.
   - Elaborate on how artists appropriate each other's work to validate and extend their ideas.
   - Explain that appropriation cannot be more than thirty percent of any given piece.

Level Three

Essential Question: How many ways can I express my ideas? (anchor Cr2)

1. **Student can develop mastery over one or more materials or techniques.**
   - Explore the variety of classroom materials and choose a favorite.
   - Engage students by asking them to repeat the same idea using a different material or by changing technique with the same material.
   - Elaborate on how changes in technique can increase control over their materials.
   - Explain that mastery of a material leads to the invention of a new techniques.

Essential Question: Which related pieces tell a story? (anchor Pr5)

2. **Student can develop a portfolio of work that shows unity and variety.**
   - Explore the idea of combining parts of different pieces to form a new piece.
   - Engage partners who will choose two of each other's previous works to combine.
   - Elaborate on the deconstruction of form to reconstruct something novel.
   - Explain that combining parts of previous work maintains unity but also creates variety.

Essential Question: What ideas can these materials represent? (anchor Re8)

3. **Student can interpret meaning from materials that relate to a subject matter.**
   - Explore how the materials communicate the subject matter in their work.
   - Engage students asking them to connect their subject matter to personal experiences.
   - Elaborate on which other materials might express the same meaning in their work.
   - Explain how materials carry meaning that help communicate their subject matter.

Essential Questions: Where can my ideas complement the work of other artists? (anchor Cn11)

4. Students can graft their ideas into social, cultural, or historical art.

- Explore timelines of social, cultural, or historical art.
- Engage students by asking them to find similarities with their own work.
- Elaborate on characteristics and attributes that identify various artistic works.
- Explain how student work can further the work of previous artists.

Level Four

Essential Question: What can I change to broaden my ideas? (anchor Cr3)

1. Student can refine ideas by changing materials and/or subject matter.

- Explore the change in an artist's style, such as Picasso's blue and rose periods.
- Engage students to number their postcards of documented work chronologically.
- Elaborate on changes throughout the portfolio with materials or subject matter.
- Explain that ideas are refined by changing something in the work to move forward in a new direction.

Essential Question: Can I arrange my work following a sequence or chronology? (anchor Pr6)

2. Student can convey a line of inquiry through a presentation of related works.

- Explore story-telling through the arrangement of portfolio works.
- Engage students to select works that are related in some way.
- Elaborate on the meaning of the selected works, presenting them in successive order.
- Explain their display of works in a written artist statement.

Essential Question: How does context change the meaning of my ideas? (anchor Re9)

3. Student can apply ideas to social contexts that will extend their meaning.

- Explore artwork from its social context, such as Bearden's *The Great Migration, 1941.*
- Engage students to connect any subject matter in their work with its context such as family, identity, race, etc.
- Elaborate on how the context for an artist's work extends the meaning of the work.
- Explain that contexts can change to alter the meaning of a subject matter.

Essential Question: How is my work unique compared to the work of other artists? (anchor Cn11)

4. Student can contribute novelty to the work of social, cultural, or historical art.

- Explore the differences between artists of the same social, cultural, or historical period.
- Engage students to list synonyms to describe their work and the work of another artist(s).

- Elaborate by listing antonyms describing differences between the same works.
- Explain that differences in their work can add novelty to the work of previous artists.

The curricular domain that most closely aligns with a student's strengths will provide the best opportunity for success in school. Because my work is in art education, I can only inference how an open curriculum might apply in other disciplines. However, all disciplines had a much broader context before American life became fragmented by our culture of mass production. Work life moved to factories and offices; religious practices stayed behind closed doors. Every part of society was separated by place and function. As such, the factory-like schools, rows of seats and mandatory curriculum began mass producing students. This tide has receded, however. An open curriculum brings together the separate domains within a curricular area providing a broader context for student engagement. Students can choose how to demonstrate what they know and can do through their strengths in one or more domain areas. Hypothetical rubrics for an open curriculum in Science, English, Math, and Social Studies can be found in the appendix.

CHAPTER SIX

Standards and Carnegie Credits

Standards are student behaviors that demonstrate evidence of higher-level thinking skills, as defined in Bloom's Taxonomy (1956), and measurable through growth. These higher-level thinking skills require students to contextualize knowledge, giving it meaning and a viewpoint that is original. Students then, who exercise choice to demonstrate a personal viewpoint are engaging with curriculum in an authentic way. Their decisions reflect the thinking processes inherent within a curricular area. The rubrics in previous chapters document the behaviors and outcomes of students that reach levels of proficiency through mastery in an art curriculum. But the first time I observed students exercising choice to demonstrate higher-level thinking was in a fourth-grade math class.

The teacher began by reviewing basic operations and equations. Then she wrote one number, "36" on the front classroom board. Students immediately began working. Some sat with a peer, but all were clear on the objective for the day. I, however, was baffled. Instead of giving her students a handout or assignment with the same formulas and grading according to the right answers, this teacher was opening the curriculum to engage all students in basic mathematical thinking. All the students were writing equations using addition, subtraction, multiplication and division that equaled "36."

The teacher walked around the room checking for understanding and answering student questions. Some were adding just two or three numbers, others made equations so long they had to turn over their paper! It was clear that all the students were exercising mathematical thinking skills, even though their formulas were different and represented varying levels of proficiency. None of the students finished the activity before the teacher went on with instruction. In addition, the teacher was able to work with students less proficient while students with above average skill created more and more complex equations. The students striving for proficiency were challenged, just as the students who exhibited mastery.

Engaging students toward mastery requires the flexibility of an open curriculum. Using this model, students schedule classes that closely align with their strengths and motivation to excel in school. When the format of a curriculum controls how knowledge must be constructed to demonstrate proficiency, we put many students at risk. Without intrinsic motivation, these students will disengage and fail. If not literally, they will certainly fail to develop confidence in their abilities or their sense of belonging in the world. Sadly, many students adapt to a "one size fits all" curriculum. They detach from their intrinsic motivation. Learning devolves into turning in assignments and passing the final exam. "Learning in order to pass a test is qualitatively different from learning for its own sake" (Kohn, 1999). But there is a better way.

Carnegie Credits provide an opportunity for all students to receive an education that motivates them to excel in school. Some educators advocate for students to achieve a Carnegie Credit when they have completed the curricular goals. Too often, however, curricular goals consist of written assignments from a course syllabus. Completing all the assignments, however, does not necessarily show evidence of proficiency, much less mastery. Standards demonstrate higher-level thinking and measures growth, not checking off course requirements. Every assignment is simply an isolated grade. Standardized assignments and tests do make comparisons between students possible and reliable. Yet herein lies the fallacy, comparing students with each other is not a baseline for measuring the growth of individual students. The math class I observed engaged students through mathematical thinking skills, not getting the right answers on an assignment or test. Those who have strengths in a curricular area can achieve mastery while others develop varying levels of proficiency during the same scheduled amount of time. There are students in my semester art classes who meet the criteria for proficiency by the end of the first quarter. But they have the potential to reach a mastery level of achievement. If I said "You can leave now, there's nothing more for you to do here" they would look at me in horror.

"What are you saying, Mrs. Chapin?!"

"Can we still come in at lunch or after school?" Students who love art never want the class to end because the success they experience in the art room gives them confidence in other areas of their lives. It is a place of belonging where their strengths are recognized and supported. The view that learning consists of how the same information can be absorbed by all the students in a determined period of time is incompatible with the use of standards. Students have the opportunity to *individualize* curriculum reaching for standards that promote rigor and higher-level thinking skills.

Chart Thirteen is a poster from my classroom that students use to identify questions related to Bloom's taxonomy. The questions begin with individual student works and increases in complexity to address how others respond to their work and where the work fits into the larger world of art. As such, the goal for students is to reach higher-level thinking which deepens and broadens their work. In some way, the taxonomy represents *hemisphericity* as much as a hierarchy. The first three levels involve deductive reasoning (left-brain) whereas the higher levels are inductive responses (right-brain) that require interpretation by the students. The hemispheres share information continuously and simultaneously.

Chart Thirteen
Prompts for Bloom's Taxonomy

Knowledge	Students can control materials and invent technique. • Which elements of art are you working with? • Where can you incorporate missing elements? • How can you combine elements within each piece?
Comprehension	Students can define problems in their work and risk "mistakes." • What problem are you trying to solve? • What information do you need to solve the problem? • Where can you find resources to continue the work?
Application	Students can express something personal in their work. • How do the elements in the work communicate your idea? • What subject matter do you see in your work? • How does the material communicate the subject matter?
Analysis	Student can identify similarities and differences in their work. • Where is the similarity between individual works? • Where can you find differences between the works? • How does the work change over time?
Synthesis	Student can combine previous works to develop their ideas. • What is your best work? • Why is it your best work? • What can you add from another piece to develop the work?
Evaluation	Student achieves the goals they intended in their work. • Where does your work connect with the history of ideas? • What has been accomplished with this idea in the past? • What can your work add to the work of previous artists?
Creation	Student work intersects with the work of previous artists. • What were you trying to express in your work? • Where can others visually read what you intended? • How do you move forward from here?

Reforms in education that continue to perpetuate a breadth approach to Carnegie Credits can undermine socio-emotional growth for many students. Limiting choice takes control away from individual students whose strengths may be less valued in our society, or whose gifts do not mature until later in life. Students are one-of-a-kind, recognizable with hair, teeth, and fingerprints that *only* identify them. Students also have a "brain-print," their intellectual DNA, from "neural pathways that have been developing since birth, which are highly individualized" (Brown, 2017). Yet students are reduced and defined by comparative categories including class rank, IQ, gender, and race. These only serve to further depersonalize their education. High school seniors graduate with a cumulative grade point average that determines their future opportunities. Many of these graduates *undervalue* their strengths and are painfully aware of their weaknesses. Curriculum must match a student's strengths so their grade point averages accurately reflect future goals and potential. If not, then equity in education is unattainable for those students.

Carnegie Credits can support student strengths and provide an individualized education for all students. Let's say, for example, a student identifies strengths in order as Math, Music, Science, Social Studies, and Visual Art. These top five domain areas should comprise the bulk of a student's course selections. Ideally, this student's graduation requirements would be 4 credits in Mathematics, 3 credits in Music, 3 credits in Science, 3 credits in Social Studies, 2 credits in Visual Art and 8 "elective" credits in remaining course selections. This individual approach to graduation credits does not suggest that a student can be non-proficient in any "elective" areas.

Our testing industry, however, has a stranglehold on scheduling courses for Carnegie Credit. Its exclusive use of numerical rankings is based on standardized tests. Student academic records exploit school districts across our nation. Ravitch (2013) writes that "Schools should treat the test scores of individual students as confidential information... as doctors maintain confidentiality about their patients' medical records." A better approach may be to open the curriculum so students can access courses that support their future goals. If we can differentiate instruction and assessment, then it must be possible to differentiate Carnegie Credits, the requirements for a high school diploma.

Most school districts have required curriculum like the State of Wisconsin. The Department of Public Instruction there recommends 23.5 credits in the following areas, though only 22 credits are required along with a Civics test. These requirements include 4 credits in English, 3 credits in Math, 3 credits in Science, 3 credits in Social Studies, 2 credits in Physical Education and Health and 8 elective credits in the arts, world languages and technology (https://dpi.wi.gov). But if most of these required credits do not align with a student's strengths, their grade point averages are unreliable predictors of success.

The idea that every student should take the same prerequisite classes *before* engaging them in areas of interest and strengths is short-sighted. In my observation of choice-based learning, just the opposite occurs. Students who discover their strengths understand how they learn and overcome their fear of failure. Jessica is a creative and productive art student who avoids drawing classes every semester. She has Scholastic awards in fiber arts and exhibits work in ceramics. Jessica prefers working with actual three-dimensional space, not the representation of space on a flat drawing surface. But one day, buoyant from achievements in fiber arts and ceramics, she takes a drawing class. Weeks later, she bursts into the ceramic studio with her sketchbook smiling from ear to ear. Jessica's strengths provide her with the confidence and motivation to seek challenges. She achieves proficiency in drawing through confidence in her past artistic success. My strong conviction is that district initiatives, including state tests scores, will improve in *direct correlation* with strengthening our students' self-efficacy, a belief in their own potential and ability to learn.

As we have seen, an open curriculum gives students the opportunity to schedule courses closely aligned with their strengths. This possibility grew out of multiple intelligences theory which has the potential to individualize curriculum for students without comparing them to others. To illustrate this, I gave two hundred and fifty-five high school students the "Adapted McKenzie (Zohar and Marshall) Multiple Intelligences Survey" (see appendix) as a baseline for inquiry. Four student responses were incomplete surveys and eliminated, leaving two hundred and fifty-one students in this study. The *McKenzie Multiple Intelligences Survey* (McKenzie 1999) is free online, permissible to print and/or modify if the copyright tag remains intact. I adapted the survey to include the spiritualist intelligence (Zohar and Marshall, 2006) because there is evidence of such subject matter in student art work. MI Research and Consulting, Inc. (Schearer, 1996) offers MIDAS, the Multiple Intelligences Developmental Assessment Scale which is a more comprehensive tool.

As in all self-reporting surveys, no answers are wrong. This is an important distinction when documenting a student's perceived strengths. Self-reporting is not an objective view of the person. It is what the *student believes* about themselves. Over time student perceptions change, so there is no need to correct them if you think they are mistaken. In addition to giving us a profile of the student's perceived strengths, we will see other areas that the student avoids. The goal of the survey is to *first* identify the areas of strengths and preferences, keeping in mind that it will only tell us how someone responds at a specific time and place. Student preferences may change over time as their work develops. Our purpose is to gather information that facilitates instruction and behavioral growth towards higher-level thinking skills. It is significant that of the two hundred and fifty-one students, no two student checklists are the same on the survey. The overall results show that only eight *pairs* of students have the same perceived strengths. In other words, on average only one other student in a classroom has similar interests and motivation as another child in the same class. Every other child has a *different* combination of perceived strengths, different ways of receiving information, and different pathways for interpreting meaning.

The survey asks students to check statements that are true for them on each of the multiple intelligence sections. One hundred and thirty-five responses had all ten statements under a section checked, suggesting strong interest and motivation in that area. Chart Fourteen shows the distribution of those scores indicating that over fifty percent of the student responses perceive their highest strengths in intrapersonal and spiritualist intelligences. Spatial and bodily kinesthetic are the next highest scores perhaps because the students are from an elective art class. As the pie chart illustrates only a combined nine percent of the students check all ten statements in mathematical-logical and verbal-linguistic strengths. Yet, those intelligences dominate our present testing of all students in K-12 education. It would be interesting to view results from students taking mandatory core curricular areas.

Chart Fourteen
Student Survey on Perceived Strengths

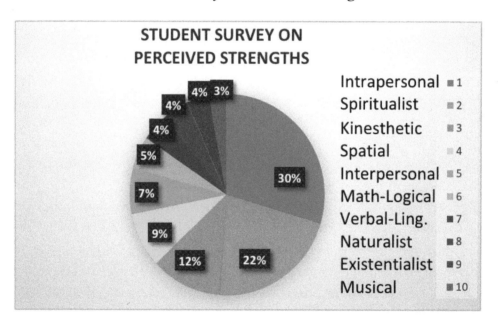

The graphs below in Chart Fifteen compare the survey responses of one individual student with the other two hundred and fifty students who successfully completed the survey. The individual student is included in a darker bar throughout each category. You will see how this student compares with the perceived strengths of peers in the same school environment. Notably, the individual student identifies strengths in only a few sections compared with peers and lacks interest in a few other sections. But most of the survey sections place the student in the average middle area of the graphs compared with peers.

Chart Fifteen
Individual Student Responses Compared with Peers

Naturalist

0	1
1	14
2	21
3	37
4	35
5	35
6	31
7	39
8	22
9	10
10	6

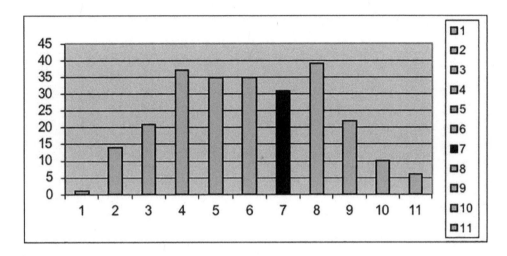

Musical

0	0
1	7
2	10
3	23
4	25
5	31
6	52
7	40
8	22
9	27
10	4

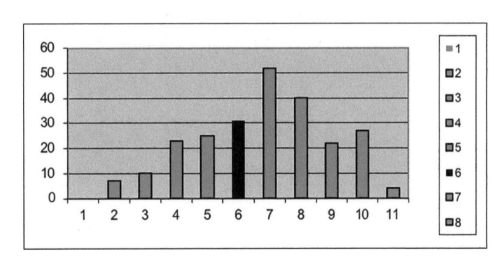

Logical

0	3
1	14
2	23
3	35
4	31
5	42
6	31
7	29
8	27
9	9
10	7

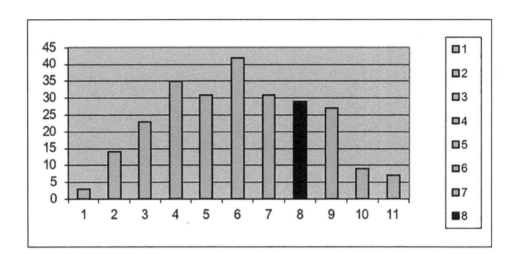

Existential

0	2
1	13
2	19
3	33
4	31
5	27
6	37
7	38
8	23
9	20
10	5

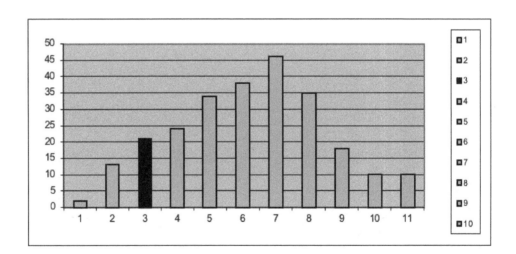

Interpersonal

0	2
1	13
2	21
3	24
4	34
5	38
6	46
7	35
8	18
9	10
10	10

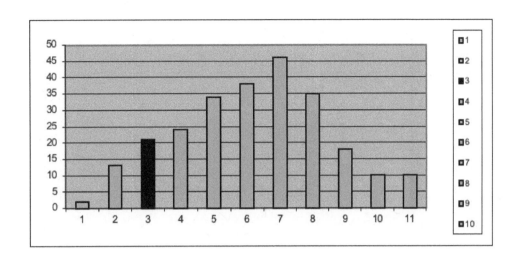

Bodily Kinesthetic

0	4
1	5
2	5
3	15
4	28
5	33
6	43
7	38
8	31
9	33
10	16

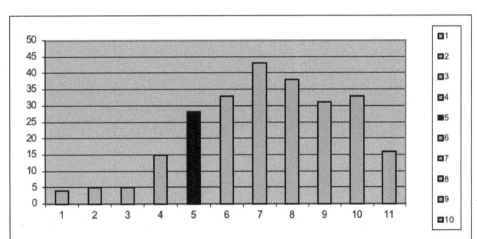

Verbal

0	6
1	23
2	26
3	41
4	32
5	42
6	33
7	20
8	15
9	7
10	6

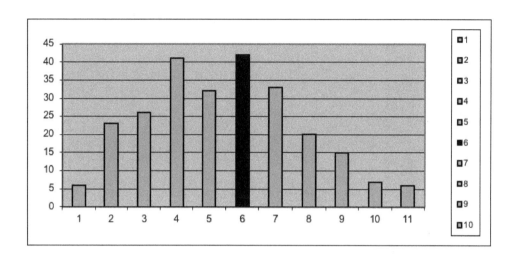

Intrapersonal

0	2
1	3
2	10
3	13
4	19
5	26
6	35
7	33
8	33
9	37
10	40

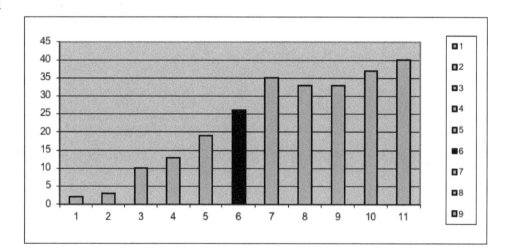

Spatial

0	2
1	9
2	11
3	17
4	39
5	35
6	53
7	28
8	30
9	15
10	12

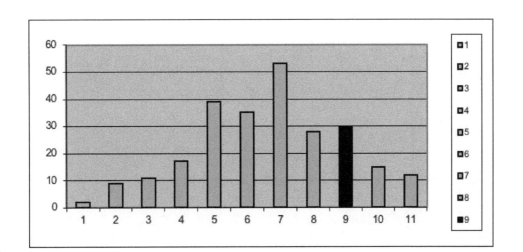

Spiritualist

0	3
1	10
2	12
3	15
4	29
5	30
6	31
7	30
8	36
9	26
10	29

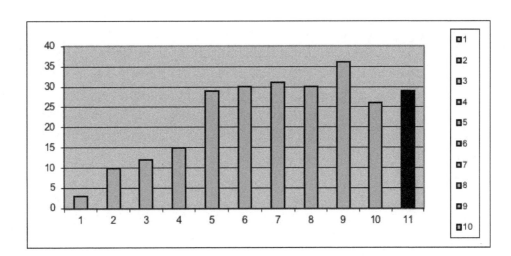

The graphs show a greater number of students in the middle range with fewer on the high or low end of each intelligence. The individual student included in the black bars demonstrates how one student can fall into higher, middle and lower categories. This is like the bell-shaped curve we use to compare and evaluate students on standardized tests including the SAT, ACT and IQ exams. We expect most students to score in the middle range with fewer students achieving higher or lower scores because the bell curve views intelligence as a fixed measure (Fletcher R. and Hattie J., 2011). Teachers are also accountable for grading on the bell curve, including by race and gender. Many students will "land in the bottom half of the bell curve because the bell curve always has a bottom half" (Ravitch, 2013). The individual student included in the black bars, however, confirms that areas of perceived strengths are not the same as most peers within the same classroom. Those are the student strengths we must align with curriculum.

The noticeable exception to the bell curve in the intelligence surveys is the eighth graph for the intrapersonal intelligence (what you are thinking or feeling). Most of the students respond with a high number of intrapersonal statements that may reflect the "identity" stage which emerges during adolescence. Spiritual intelligence in the tenth graph also has less of a bell curve for which I have no explanation. To conclude, most students believe themselves to have higher than average scores in a few intelligences, average in others, and show little interest in some. While few will have the exact same graphs from the survey, all the students will show areas of interest higher than their peers. It is those areas of strengths that should be reflected in an individual student's Carnegie Credit requirements.

Chart Sixteen is an Open Curriculum model for course selections at the secondary high school level. Social Studies bring the strengths of *interpersonal* students to Economics, Geography, Civics, and History, all records of human interactions and events. Subsequent curricula build upon each other following their corollary intelligences. Students high in *intrapersonal* intelligence will be drawn to domains concerning the individual, such as Health and Psychology. Sports, Dance, and Drama all involve the *bodily kinesthetic* intelligence expressing tactile movement in space. Music, Art, and Culinary courses attract students who are highly *sensory* through sight, sound, texture, taste, and smell. Symbolic representation of these sensory experiences is *logical-linguistic*, students who find strengths in Math and Languages (English, ASL, and other world languages), including Debate. The *naturalist* intelligence is high in students drawn to the Sciences, Industry and Technology including Agriculture, Industrial Arts, Business, and Computer Science. The *existential* intelligence supports courses in Philosophy, Ethics, and Law. And the *spiritualist* intelligence nurtures the study of Mindfulness and World Religions.

Chart Sixteen
The Open Curriculum Model

INTERPERSONAL
**Social Studies
Curriculum**

Economics/Geography
Civics/History

INTRAPERSONAL
Health/Psychology

BODILY-KINESTHETIC
Sports/Dance/Drama

SENSORY
Music/Arts/Culinary

LOGICAL-LINGUISTIC
Math/Languages/Debate

NATURALIST
Sciences/Industry/Technology

EXISTENTIALIST
Philosophy/Ethics/Law

SPIRITUALIST
Mindfulness/World Religions

Brown University, in Providence, Rhode Island, removed general course requirements for entering freshman fifty years ago. Their philosophy called the *Open Curriculum* engages students immediately with courses in their areas of interest. Two courses per semester must include a writing component. Grades are pass or fail. And students can change schedules in response to a change in their career plans. Scheduling classes that individualize curriculum integrates cognitive and socio-emotional learning. Students can choose curricula that best promotes their strengths. An individualized curriculum is a multi-faceted approach to learning that meets the diverse student needs in our schools. As a result, Carnegie Credits can support growth for all students in an open curriculum.

We know that education for this generation must be flexible and sustainable. But education is not just about "what you know and can do" to get a job or jump from one profession to another when a job terminates. It is also about maintaining a sense of equilibrium and purpose during life changes. It is about knowing yourself, your strengths, beliefs, and values. Enlightenment writers like Voltaire and Rousseau envisioned a utopia where society existed for the good of the individual, who in turn reciprocated by *choosing* to do good for the larger community. In practice, however, political and economic realities have trumped our social sense of the greater good. Educating for competition in global markets that deplete the world's resources, for example, is self-defeating. When markets drive education, opportunities are limited to those who profit from such a wager. The next generation will inherit both the challenges and opportunities that we are leaving behind.

After starting my family, I returned to teaching at the Brookline Elementary Teacher Center in Pittsburgh, PA, a pilot program for the Pittsburgh Research-Based Instructional and Supervisory Model (PRISM). One day as I ran through the rain, a smiling man stood opening the door to the school building for me. He was wearing a plaid shirt, work pants, and boots. I thanked him and thought, "What a nice custodian." While in my art classroom, he stopped by to check on me. Since it was my first day, I took the time before classes to prepare materials for the kids. But during the morning classes, the custodian again walked into the art room. Students stopped working and sat perfectly straight and still. He walked slowly between the rows. He stopped at one student's desk and gave him a small piece of paper. The student quickly scribbled on the paper and returned it. Then the custodian put a dollar on the student's desk and walked out of the room. The kids cheered! The student received a dollar for the correct answer on a math problem! While the student engagement was awesome, I had mixed feelings about a custodian interrupting classwork. So, before leaving school, I went to the office to meet the principal and planned to mention the incident.

Yes, it was the *principal* in a plaid shirt wearing work pants and boots! I learned more than I taught that day. This principal did not sit in an office with ongoing administrative tasks. He is serving students, teachers, and the community as a *coworker*. None of us can reform education alone. Isolated areas of the brain may be responsible for distinct capabilities, but the most significant discovery in brain research is that those separate domains share information. Human intelligence is functionally symbiotic, just as our society reflects the shared experiences of everyone. Dedicated teachers, administrators, and parents in collaboration can bring about the educational reforms our students deserve.

Teaching through the context of each student, modifying instruction, and differentiating curriculum *provides* the equity model we have been seeking in education. Formative rubrics that include behaviors for self-efficacy ensure the success of an open curriculum. Equality means that all have the freedom to *choose* their opportunities. Our objective is clear: we educate so students can make the best decisions for themselves and others. Education is a choice that individuals initiate but society must nurture. The same possibilities that the educator John Dewey observed in students of the late 19th century remain true today.

"The child's own instincts and powers furnish the material and give the starting point for all education. Save as the efforts of the educator to connect with some activity which the child is carrying on of his own initiative independent of the educator, education becomes reduced to a pressure from without. It may, indeed, give certain external results, but cannot truly be called educative. Without insight into the psychological structured activities of the individual, the educative process will, therefore, be haphazard and arbitrary. If it chances to coincide with the child's activity it will get leverage; if it does not, it will result in friction, or disintegration, or the arrest of development" (John Dewey: 1897).

CHAPTER SEVEN

The Nature of Cyclical Learning

All social institutions and individuals undergo cyclical change. Early photography in the nineteenth century replaced painting as a primary way to create realistic images. In response, artists explored Expressionism which focuses on the emotional state of the artist as subject matter, such as the Fauvist paintings of blue horses by Franz Marc. The viewer was brought out of the natural world and into an imaginative world of feeling and form. Artists then explored Abstraction so the viewer could identify with the emotional content in the work. Pablo Picasso's *Weeping Woman*, for example, could be any woman experiencing grief because she is not recognizable as a specific person. Finally, a true break with Realism occurs in Non-representational art where the subject matter disappears into elemental fragments detached from the material world, spiritual in nature, as Wassily Kandinsky would say. Non-Representational artists must return to Realism, then, to gather more forms and patterns that can again be fused with emotion, abstracted and become detached from its place and time. The cycle repeats itself from Realism to Expressionism to Abstraction and Non-Representationalism throughout the history of art.

My thoughts on the cycles of life-long learning are like the phases of changing styles in visual art. The drawing in Chart Seventeen pulls us into the circumference of a circle, the interface between an individual and their environment. Following an inward spiral movement, the learner can pass through successive stages of receiving information, choosing relevance, producing work, constructing meaning, developing ideas and resolving conflicts in the work to create something novel. At any time, an individual can cycle back outwards past previous stages of growth to gather new information, then moving inward again through the same neural pathways.

The model also illustrates how the multiple intelligences may facilitate this cyclical movement, going back to correct or retrieve information from previous learning stored in memory. The chart shows the *personal* intelligences incorporating knowledge from the environment. The *bodily kinesthetic* intelligence then screens the information in space and time to decide what is relevant. The sensory intelligences produce outcomes that are visual, auditory, etc. in response to new information. From those experiences, the *logical-linguistic* intelligences attach personal meaning symbolically to our memories. The *naturalist* intelligence reconstructs ideas out of those meaningful experiences. *Existential* intelligence identifies paradox, ideas that are in conflict and seek resolution. And spiritualist intelligence creates novelty by combining multiple viewpoints to form new knowledge.

Chart Seventeen
Cyclical Nature of Learning

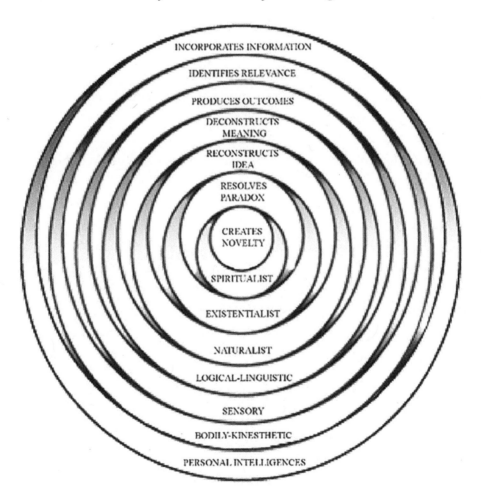

Technology accelerates the need for students to adapt to changing environments. Adaptation, then, is also a cyclical process where the multiple intelligences deconstruct and reconstruct knowledge in response to a new environment. These cycles dip into our reservoir of memory continually refining and updating knowledge, letting go of knowledge that is no longer useful or true. This view is consistent with research on multiple intelligences showing that they do not function independently but share and translate information (Genç, 2011).

Seeing the multiple intelligences model within Erikson's socio-emotional model makes it possible to view Gardner's theory as a hierarchy. It may be that the multiple intelligences emerge or mature *during* a stage crisis of socio-emotional development. And, as the intelligences are present in nascent form at birth, socio-emotional stages may also be encoded in human memory. The inference is that cognitive and socio-emotional growth are inextricably linked. Chart Eighteen visualizes the possibility of various intelligences emerging throughout human development. The correlations suggest that an ongoing dialogue between the personal intelligences receives and stores information from the environment. Together they form our comprehension and ability to find relevant information for decision-making. Mental schemas of these choices remain in memory, accessible at any time. Maturation occurs when memory schemas deconstruct to incorporate new information or a changing perspective. Identity, a sense of belonging, follows while developing our potential strengths. As we age and face paradoxes, our worldview broadens with nuance and novelty. These are all social adaptations to more complex interactions with the interpersonal environment (Pinker, 2003).

Sometimes, when I close my eyes and remember students who have walked through the art room, I can still see all the intelligences. Roarke sits and bows his head as if in meditation while Jesse ruminates over his work. Amanda has earbuds, listening to music. Tabitha chooses a seat near the window with the open sky, next to my plants. Justin collects and arranges the same tools in the same way to begin his work. Doug walks around and around and then exits to the bathroom, seemingly on a quest. Jenna sits next to her best friend, lost in conversation. Ray has his nose in a book reading while Damen doodles in his sketchbook. Somehow, curriculum must shape itself around all these individual differences. It is important here to note the work of Kurt Goldstein (1939), a pioneer in neuropsychology, who cautions that education should not destroy or lose the individual's integrity. Furthermore, he predicts that change in an individual by environmental stimuli must be "equalized after a definite time, so that the organism regains that 'average' state which corresponds to its nature." This is consistent with the socio-emotional model of development and the multiple intelligences framework for growth. Every student has a set point, a homeostasis that determines resilience and adaptability. Implications for future research on the states of equilibrium that we achieve in learning would be enlightening.

The heart of any theory is an idea, a seed with potential for growth that just needs to root at the right time and in the right place. My book hopes to achieve that inevitable outcome, bearing the fruit

Chart Eighteen
Erikson and Gardner Models

Spiritualist
EGO-INTEGRITY VS. DESPAIR   WISDOM

OLDER ADULTHOOD
60's and 70's

GENERATIVITY VS. STAGNATION

Existentialist
CARING

MIDDLE ADULTHOOD
40's and 50's

INTIMACY VS. ISOLATION

YOUNG ADULTHOOD
20's and 30's

Naturalist
LOVE

EGO-IDENTITY VS. ROLE CONFUSION

Verbal- Mathematical-

L Linguistic Logical

ADOLESCENCE
12-18 years

FIDELITY

COMPETENCE

LATENCY
7-12 years

Musical Spatial

INDUSTRY VS. INFERIORITY

PURPOSE

Bodily-Kinesthetic

GENITAL-
LOCOMOTIVE
3-6 years

INITIATIVE VS. GUILT

WILL

Intrapersonal

ANAL 18 months
to 3 years

AUTONOMY VS. SELF-DOUBT

HOPE

Interpersonal
TRUST VS. MISTRUST

ORAL 0-18 months

of countless hours of observation and instruction, monitoring, and measuring student achievement. During my last year before retirement, a student shared with me the image below. It is a picture she took of her hand reflecting the word HOPE in a car's side-view mirror. On the mirror are the words "Objects in mirror are closer than they appear." This is one of the many gifts from students that I treasure. Hope does indeed feel closer than it appears. May this be true for our students, teachers, schools, and communities.

Photograph by Ninth Grader

EPILOGUE

The hallway is long and dark, shrouded by lockers and muted in color. The wooden floorboards glisten like waves with a smooth and worn surface that dip and rise from decades of use. The windows are tall and wide like my mother's lap beckoning me to come and sit on her sills to bask in sunlight. This is my classroom. Here I follow those who taught before me, upholding the greatest social reform movement in human history---public education. For knowledge belongs to all, irrespective of age, gender, race, religion or money. And yet, the profound implications of equity in education have yet to be realized.

Virtual experiences that are as real, and for some students more real, than their everyday lives are filling in the vacuum. As in the fifteenth century we are sending explorers out to sea not knowing if they will fall over that edge when they reach the horizon line. The vast expanse of knowledge surrounding them compels us to face the question of relevance. Long before written and tested curriculum became the focus of instruction, learning came from a connection to our communities. Artists, for example, teach us to respond to beauty. Mathematicians explain the constructs of space and time invisible to others. When we ask students to screen for what is relevant they connect with an idea within a classroom environment. Relevance, then, is based on the choices students make in that curriculum to direct their own learning. Equity is realized when every student can not only survive but thrive in our schools.

The history of education shows that integrative educative theories can create diverse pathways to achievement. Erikson's research focuses on individuals as they adapt to changing environments. The socio-emotional needs of students as they navigate those changes must take precedence over curricular goals. Gardner's model recognizes the wide diversity of intelligences, providing teachers with varied methodologies for student engagement and motivation. And Bloom's taxonomy directs curricular goals towards higher level-thinking skills. At present, our best practices come from utilizing integrative educative theories appropriate to the needs and goals of individual students. Teachers who use flexible methods and employ varied theories are creating opportunities for all their students.

Chart Nineteen shows some correlations between the three cognitive and behavioral models that reflect both academic and socio-emotional learning. I modified Bloom's taxonomy to include creation of knowledge as a final developmental stage; after remembering, understanding, applying, analyzing, synthesizing, and evaluating. I do *not* move synthesis, as in the Anderson and Krathwohl model (2011), because the choice-based student portfolios clearly demonstrate that analysis and synthesis are separate and consecutive stages. Evaluation involves identifying the work of previous historical persons or trends that validates a student's work and inquiry. And creation of new knowledge occurs when student work adds a novel piece or interpretation to recognized historical work in a particular domain.

Chart Nineteen
Integrative Educative Theories

Cognitive-Behavioral Outcomes	Source of Knowledge	Adaptive Strengths (Erikson)	Emerging Intelligences (Gardner)	Cognitive-Behavioral (Bloom)
Students explore classroom environments.	Observation	Trust (vs. mistrust/ uncertainty)	Interpersonal	Environment (source of information)
Students recognize ideas from intrinsic motivation.	Imagination	Autonomy (vs. self-doubt)	Intrapersonal	Knowledge (Receives information)
Students choose resources from classroom to express ideas.	Media Preferences	Initiative (vs. guilt/mistakes)	Bodily-Kinesthetic	Comprehension (Understands relevance)
Students produce and document outcomes.	Subject matter Preferences	Competence (vs. inferiority)	Sensory-Memory	Application (Produces outcomes)
Students connect work to personal experiences.	Whole Group Instruction	Identity (vs. rejection)	Logical- Linguistic	Analysis (Deconstructs meaning)

Students extend meaning in work to include social contexts.	Small Group Instruction	Intimacy (vs. loneliness)	Naturalist	Synthesis (Reconstructs ideas)
Students find a social, cultural, or historical context for their work.	Individual Instruction	Generativity (vs. indifference)	Existentialist	Evaluation (Resolves paradox)
Students adds novelty to social, cultural, or historical works.	Student-Guided Inquiry	Wisdom (vs. hopelessness)	Spiritualist	Creation (New Knowledge)

The above "map" shows where we are and where we have been over the past seventy-five years of research in education. The research, however, takes too long to trickle down into practice resulting in significant lag time and costly corrective measures. This is particularly true when the research comes from outside the classroom setting. The increasing role of teachers as researchers supported by National Board Certification, can speed up that timeline. Colleagues were shocked when the art teacher, me, received the first National Board Certification in our district. Only the principal understood the accomplishment and he changed the marquis in the front of the high school to say, "Ms. Chapin receives first National Board Certification!"

Three days later, the marquis was replaced with a sports event. Some teachers were concerned that it looked to the community as though the high school had only one qualified teacher. Still, I appreciated the brief moment in the sun and didn't hesitate when the certificate expired ten years later to reapply for National Board Certification. The process provides feedback that is more accurate than any other form of evaluation I had received in education. My exam was scored by other art educators who never met me yet recognized my strengths in aesthetics and the history of art. That affirmation gave me confidence, the self-efficacy to teach through my strengths. The National Board for Professional Teaching Standards puts control for certification into the hands of teachers to monitor the profession, just as the open curriculum gives students control over their own learning.

Public education was founded on one basic principle, to seek the greatest good for the greatest number. Johns Hopkins University had a sign on the School of Medicine building that read "Saving Lives: One at a Time." Directly across the street on the School of Public Health building another sign hung "Saving Lives: Millions at a Time." Almost *fifty million* American students attend public schools, where *all students* are accepted. Many believe solving the inequities in public health, public welfare or public education is an impossible dream, but don't BLINK! The next generation of teachers are here and their connection to the wider world brings a passion for equity and justice. They are ready and waiting for the opportunity to prove that anything is possible if we believe in each other and especially in our kids.

I leave young art educators with these three quotes by Albert Einstein. "Imagination is more important than knowledge," "Imagination is the highest form of research," and "I want to know God's thoughts… the rest are details." I'll see you on the journey.

APPENDIX

Adapted McKenzie (Zohar and Marshall) Multiple Intelligences Survey

Multiple Intelligences Survey

© 1999 Walter McKenzie, adapted by Marlene Chapin (Zohar and Marshall, 2006)

Part I

Complete each section by placing a "1" next to each statement you feel accurately describes you. If you do not identify with a statement, leave the space provided blank. Then total the column in each section.

Section 1

_____ I enjoy categorizing things by common traits.

_____ Ecological issues are important to me.

_____ Classification helps me make sense of new data.

_____ I enjoy working in a garden.

_____ I believe preserving our National Parks is important.

_____ Putting things in hierarchies makes sense to me.

_____ Animals are important in my life.

_____ My home has a recycling system in place.

_____ I enjoy studying biology, botany and/or zoology.

_____ I pick up on subtle differences in meaning.

_____ TOTAL for Section 1

Section 2

_____ I easily pick up on patterns.

_____ I focus in on noise and sounds.

_____ Moving to a beat is easy for me.

_____ I enjoy making music.

_____ I respond to the cadence of poetry.

_____ I remember things by putting them in a rhyme.

_____ Concentration is difficult for me if there is background noise.

_____ Listening to sounds in nature can be very relaxing.

_____ Musicals are more engaging to me than dramatic plays.

_____ Remembering song lyrics is easy for me.

_____ TOTAL for Section 2

Section 3

_____ I am known for being neat and orderly.

_____ Step-by-step directions are a big help.

_____ Problem solving comes easily to me.

_____ I get easily frustrated with disorganized people.

_____ I can complete calculations quickly in my head.

_____ Logic puzzles are fun.

_____ I can't begin an assignment until I have all my "ducks in a row."

_____ Structure is a good thing.

_____ I enjoy troubleshooting something that isn't working properly.

_____ Things have to make sense to me or I am dissatisfied.

_____ TOTAL for Section 3

Section 4

_____ It is important to see my role in the "big picture" of things.

_____ I enjoy discussing questions about life.

_____ Religion is important to me.

_____ I enjoy viewing artwork.

_____ Relaxation and meditation exercises are rewarding to me.

_____ I like traveling to visit inspiring places.

_____ I enjoy reading philosophers.

_____ Learning new things is easier when I see their real-world application.

_____ I wonder if there are other forms of intelligent life in the universe.

_____ It is important for me to feel connected to people, ideas, and beliefs.

_____ TOTAL for Section 4

Section 5

_____ I learn best interacting with others.

_____ I enjoy informal chat and serious discussion.

_____ The more the merrier.

_____ I often serve as a leader among peers and colleagues.

_____ I value relationships more than ideas or accomplishments.

_____ Study groups are very productive for me.

_____ I am a "team player."

_____ Friends are important to me.

_____ I belong to more than three clubs or organizations.

_____ I dislike working alone.

_____ TOTAL for Section 5

S

Section 6

_____ I learn by doing.

_____ I enjoy making things with my hands.

_____ Sports are a part of my life.

_____ I use gestures and nonverbal cues when I communicate.

_____ Demonstrating is better than explaining.

_____ I love to dance.

_____ I like working with tools.

_____ Inactivity can make me more tired than being very busy.

_____ Hands-on activities are fun.

_____ I live an active lifestyle.

_____ TOTAL for Section 6

Section 7

_____ Foreign languages interest me.

_____ I enjoy reading books, magazines, and websites.

_____ I keep a journal.

_____ Word puzzles like crosswords or jumbles are enjoyable.

_____ Taking notes helps me remember and understand.

_____ I faithfully contact friends through letters and/or email.

_____ It is easy for me to explain my ideas to others.

_____ I write for pleasure.

_____ Puns, anagrams, and spoonerisms are fun.

_____ I enjoy public speaking and participating in debates.

_____ TOTAL for Section 7

Section 8

_____ My attitude affects how I learn.

_____ I like to be involved in causes that help others.

_____ I am keenly aware of my moral beliefs.

_____ I learn best when I have an emotional attachment to the subject.

_____ Fairness is important to me.

_____ Social justice issues interest me.

_____ Working alone can be just as productive as working in a group.

_____ I need to know why I should do something before I agree to do it.

_____ When I believe in something, I give more effort toward it.

_____ I am willing to protest or sign a petition to right a wrong.

_____ TOTAL for Section 8

Section 9

_____ I can visualize ideas in my mind.

_____ Rearranging a room and redecorating are fun for me.

_____ I enjoy creating my own works of art.

_____ I remember better using graphic organizers.

_____ I enjoy all kinds of entertainment media.

_____ Charts, graphs, and tables help me interpret data.

_____ A music video can make me more interested in a song.

_____ I can recall things as mental pictures.

_____ I am good at reading maps and blueprints.

_____ Three dimensional puzzles are fun.

_____ TOTAL for Section 9

Section 10

_____ I like to be spontaneous, living in, and being responsive to the moment.

_____ I live according to principles and beliefs and act accordingly.

_____ I have a sense of connectedness and belonging in the universe.

_____ I value other people for their differences.

_____ I can stand against the crowd and have my own convictions.

_____ I believe that I am a player in a larger drama, that I have a purpose in the world.

_____ I tend to ask "Why?" questions and need to get to the bottom of things.

_____ I like to stand back from a situation or problem and see problems in a wider context.

_____ I learn and grow from mistakes, setbacks, and suffering.

_____ There is a sense of vocation in my life where I will give back to others.

_____ TOTAL for Section 10

Part II

Now carry forward your total from each section and multiply by 10 below: Section	Total Forward	Multiply	Score
	1	X10	
	2	X10	
	3	X10	
	4	X10	
	5	X10	
	6	X10	
	7	X10	
	8	X10	
	9	X10	
	10	X10	

Part III

Now plot your scores on the bar graph provided:

100										
90										
80										
70										
60										
50										
40										
30										
20										
10										
0	Sec 1	Sec 2	Sec 3	Sec 4	Sec 5	Sec 6	Sec 7	Sec 8	Sec 9	Sec 10

Part IV
Key:

Section 1—This reflects your Naturalist strength.

Section 2—This suggests your Musical strength.

Section 3—This indicates your Logical strength.

Section 4—This illustrates your Existential strength.

Section 5—This shows your Interpersonal strength.

Section 6—This tells your Kinesthetic strength.

Section 7—This indicates your Verbal strength.

Section 8—This reflects your Intrapersonal strength.

Section 9—This suggests your Visual strength.

Section 10—This suggests your Spiritualist strength.

Chapter Charts

Rubrics for Core Academic Areas

National Standards for Science

STANDARDS CRITERIA	Advanced Evidence	Accomplished Evidence	Proficient Evidence	Some Evidence	Pts.
EARTH AND SPACE SCIENCES *Factual Reasoning* "Environment"	Student can convey societal obligations to explore and conserve our environments. *How can my experiments help sustain life in the universe? (anchor ESS3)*	Student can develop related experiments on human activity from personal experience. *What ideas can modify human activity to support life on Earth? (anchor ESS3)*	Student can research the Earth-spheres that produce our environments. *Which of my experiments are related to various Earth spheres? (anchor ESS2)*	Student can analyze the interactions of matter in their environment. *Which interactions are of interest to me? (anchor ESS1)*	
PHYSICAL SCIENCES *Conceptual Reasoning* "Energy"	Student can apply line of inquiry that shows complex applications. *How can wave technology support society with innovation? (anchor PS4)*	Student can interpret meaning from the effects of energy on matter. *Can my research show the relation between matter and energy? (anchor PS3)*	Student can analyze qualities of various forces of motion and stability within an experiment. *Which qualities of matter do I find most interesting? (anchor PS2)*	Student can express their ideas about matter in their environment. *Do I recognize my own thoughts and feelings? (anchor PS1)*	

LIFE SCIENCES *Procedural Reasoning* "Evolution"	Student can demonstrate how their organism(s) change within biological evolution. *Where can I see unity/ diversity in biological evolution?* *(anchor LS4)*	Student can trace the heredity and variation of traits for their organism(s). *How many variations of the organism(s) can I document?* *(anchor LS3)*	Student can research the ecosystems relevant for their organism(s). *What ecosystems relate to these organisms?* *(anchor LS2)*	Student can generate ideas from exploring the structure/ processes of living organisms. *Which organisms are interesting to me?* *(anchor LS1)*
ENGINEERING SCIENCES *Metacognitive Reasoning* "Applications"	Student can contribute novelty to engineering, technology or social sciences. *How is my work unique compared to the work of other scientists?* *(anchor ETS2)*	Students can graft their ideas into engineering, technology or social sciences. *Where can my ideas complement the work of other scientists?* *(anchor ETS2*	Student can synthesize their research with the work of another scientist(s). *How can my research show the influence of other scientists?* *(anchor ETS1)*	Student can relate their own ideas with the work of recognized scientists. *Where do my experiments fit with previous scientists?* *(anchor ETS1)*
			TOTAL POINTS	

Grading scores, A 13-16, B 9-12, C 5-8, Insufficient evidence 1-4

National Standards for English

STANDARDS CRITERIA	Advanced Evidence	Accomplished Evidence	Proficient Evidence	Some Evidence	Pts.
LANGUAGE *Factual Reasoning* "Grammar/ Spelling"	Student can convey a line of inquiry through a presentation of related writings. *Can I arrange my work following a sequence or chronology? (anchor 9-12 L)*	Student can develop a portfolio of writing that unifies subject matter with intent. *Which pieces are related in some way? (anchor 5-8 L)*	Student can interpret meaning and relatedness through syntax in their writing. *Which pieces tell a story? (anchor 2-4 L)*	Student can analyze the grammar and spelling in their writing. *What do I want to learn to write about? (anchor K-1 L)*	
SPEAKING AND LISTENING *Conceptual Reasoning* "Communicate Collaborate"	Student can apply ideas to social contexts that will extend their meaning. *How does context change the meaning of an idea or topic? (anchor 9-12SL*	Student can interpret meaning from discussion/topic that relates to personal experience. *What ideas do these topics unearth for me? (anchor 5-8 SL)*	Student can analyze qualities in classroom discussion and topics. *Do I agree, disagree or am I neutral on this topic? (anchor 2-4 SL)*	Student can express their thoughts/feelings in response to the classroom environment. *Do I recognize my own thoughts and feelings? (anchor K-1 SL)*	

WRITING *Procedural Reasoning* "Generate Ideas/Define Genres"	Student can refine ideas by changing genres and/or subject matter. *What can I change to broaden my ideas?* *(anchor 9-12 W*	Student can develop mastery over one or more subject matter or genres. *How many ways can I express my ideas?* *(anchor 5-8 W)*	Student can organize writing based on subject matter preferences. *What subject matter relates to these genres?* *(anchor 2-4 W)*	Student can generate ideas from exploring literary genres. *What genres are most interesting to me?* *(anchor K-1 W)*	
READING *Metacognitive Reasoning* "Connect Writing with Appropriate Authors"	Student can contribute novelty to the work of other authors. *How is my work unique compared to the work of other authors?* *(anchor 9-12 RI)*	Students can graft their ideas into a literary genre(s). *Where can my ideas complement the work of other authors?* *(anchor 5-8 RI)*	Student can synthesize their work with the work of another author(s). *How can my writing show an influence from other authors?* *(anchor 2-4 RL)*	Student can see their own ideas in the work of recognized authors. *Where do my interests fit with previous authors?* *(anchor k-1 RL)*	
				TOTAL POINTS	

Grading scores, A 13-16, B 9-12, C 5-8, Insufficient evidence 1-4

National Standards for Mathematics

STANDARDS CRITERIA	Advanced Evidence	Accomplished Evidence	Proficient Evidence	Some Evidence	Pts.
ARITHMETIC *Factual Reasoning* "Basic Number Theory/ Operations"	Student can convey a line of inquiry through multiple operations. *Can I use basic operations to explain natural/ social event(s)? (anchor9-12NBT)*	Student can use operations to create ratios and proportional relationships. *Which problems are related in some way? (anchor 5-8RP)*	Student can interpret meaning or relatedness between numeri-cal operations. *What equa-tions can express my ideas? (anchor 2-4 EE)*	Student can analyze numbers in groups and problem solve. *What are my problem-solv-ing strategies? (anchor K-1 CC)*	
GEOMETRY *Conceptual Reasoning* "Measurement of Spatial Quantities"	Student can apply ideas to social contexts that will extend their meaning. *How does context change the mean-ing of my ideas? (anchor 9-12 G)*	Student can interpret mean-ing from spatial relationships that are personal. *What ideas can these spatial relationships represent? (anchor 5-8 G)*	Student can analyze qualities in classroom materials and resources. *What forms or spaces are interest-ing to me? (anchor 2-4 G)*	Student can ex-press their ideas in response to a classroom envi-ronment. *Can I recognize my own ideas in the classroom resources or materials? (anchor K-1 NBT)*	

ALGEBRA *Procedural Reasoning* "Measurement of Unknown Quantities"	Student can refine ideas by changing materials and/or functions. *What can I change to broaden my ideas?* *(anchor 9-12 OA)*	Student can develop mastery over one or more functions. *How many ways can I express these functions?* *(anchor 5-8 OA)*	Student can organize materials based on preferences. *What functions can I express with these materials?* *(anchor 2-4 OA)*	Student can generate ideas from exploring classroom resources and Materials. *What resources/materials are interesting to me?* *(anchor K-1 NBT)*
CALCULUS/ ANALYTIC NUMBER THEORY: *Metacognitive Reasoning* "Measurement of Changing Quantities"	Student can contribute novelty to the work of previous mathematicians. *How is my work unique compared with other mathematicians?* *(anchor 9-12SP)*	Students can graft their ideas into social, cultural, or historical contexts. *Where can my ideas complement the work of another mathematician?* *(anchor 5-8 SP*	Student can synthesize their work with the work of another mathematician. *How can my work show influence from other mathematicians?* *(anchor 2-4MD*	Student can relate their own work with the work of recognized mathematicians. *Where does my work fit in with previous mathematicians?* *(anchor K-1MD)*
			TOTAL POINTS	

Grading scores, A 13-16, B 9-12, C 5-8, Insufficient evidence 1-4

National Standards for Social Studies

STANDARDS CRITERIA	Advanced Evidence	Accomplished Evidence	Proficient Evidence	Some Evidence	Pts.
GEOGRAPHY *Factual Reasoning* "Populations/Environments"	Student can convey a line of inquiry through patterns of change in society. *How does population or migration change environments? (anchors 9-12G)*	Student can demonstrate unity and variety within geographic cultures. *How can I show our diversity and commonality? (anchors 6-8 G)*	Student can interpret relatedness in populations/environments. *Which people and/or places relate in some way? (anchors 3-5 G)*	Student can analyze geographical maps. *Where would I choose a geographic location? (anchors K-2G)*	
ECONOMICS *Conceptual Reasoning* "Micro/Macro Development/Exchanges"	Student can apply ideas to social contexts that will extend their meaning. *How does development affect societal values? (anchors 9-12 E)*	Student can interpret meaning from exchanges that relate to personal experience. *What ideas can exchanges represent? (anchors 6-8 E)*	Student can analyze qualities of micro/macro development. *Does context change the meaning of monetary values? (anchors 3-5 E)*	Student can express their personal views on monetary values. *What values do I attribute to money? (anchors K-2 E)*	

CIVICS/ GOVERNMENT *Procedural Reasoning* "Virtues and Democratic Principles"	Student can refine ideas by changing principles and/ or materials. *What can I change to broaden my ideas?* *(anchors 9-12C)*	Student can develop mastery over one or more democratic principles. *How many ways can I express my ideas?* *(anchors 6-8 C)*	Student can organize materials based on subject matter principles. *What ideas can I relate to these materials/ principles?* *(anchors 3-5 C)*	Student can generate ideas from exploring classroom resources and materials. *What democratic principles are interesting to me?* *(anchors K-2 C*	
HISTORY *Metacognitive Reasoning* "Change, Continuity and Context"	Student can contribute novelty to the work of other historians. *How is my work different from other historians?* *(anchors 9-12 H)*	Students can graft their ideas into an historical viewpoint. *Where can my ideas complement the work of other historians?* *(anchors 6-8 H)*	Student can synthesize their interest(s) with historical periods. *How has this aspect changed over time?* *(anchors 3-5 H)*	Student can relate their interests with some aspect of history. *What aspect(s) of history am I most interested in?* *(anchors K-2 H)*	
				TOTAL POINTS	

Grading scores, A 13-16, B 9-12, C 5-8, Insufficient evidence 1-4

REFERENCES

Ainsworth, Larry and Viegut, Donald. *Common Formative Assessments*. Corwin Press, SAGE Publications, 2006.

Albrecht, Karl. *Practical Intelligence*. John Wiley & Sons, 2007.

Anderson, Lorin and Krathwohl, David, et al (Eds.) *A Taxonomy for Learning, Teaching, and Assessing: A Revision of Bloom's Taxonomy of Educational Objectives (abridged edition)*. Boston: Pearson Education Group, 2001.

Armstrong, Thomas. *Multiple Intelligences in the Classroom*. Alexandria: Association for Supervision and Curriculum Development, 2018.

Arnheim, Rudolph. *Visual Thinking*. University of California, Berkley and Los Angeles, 1969.

Bandura, Albert. *Self-Efficacy: The Exercise of Control*. New York, NY: Freeman, 1997.

Baumeister, Roy and Bushman, Brad. *Social Psychology and Human Nature, Comprehensive Edition.*, Boston MA: Cengage Learning, 2014.

Beck, Walter. *Self-Development in Drawing*. Putnam's Sons: London, 1928.

Benware, Carl and Deci, Edward. *"The Quality of Learning with an Active Versus Passive Motivational Set." American Education Research Journal*. 1984 (21): 755-765.

Black, Paul and Wiliam, Dylan. "The Formative Purpose: Assessment must first promote learning," pp.20-50. In Mark Wilson, (Ed.), *103rd Yearbook of the National Society for the Study of Education, Part II*. Chicago: University of Chicago Press, 2004.

Bloom, Benjamin. S. et al. *The Taxonomy of Educational Objectives, Handbook I: The Cognitive Domain*. New York: David McKay Co., Inc, 1956.

Brooks, Jacqueline, and M. *In Search of Understanding: The Case for Constructivist Classrooms*. Alexandria, VA: Association For Supervision and Curriculum Development, 1993.

Brown, Brené. *Daring Greatly: How the Courage to be Vulnerable Transforms the Way to Live, Love Parent and Lead*. New York: Penguin Random House, 2015.

Bybee, Rodger W. *BSCS 5E Instructional Model: Creating Teachable Moments*. Arlington, VA: NSTA Press, 2015.

Campbell, Joseph. edited by Kudler, D. *The Symbol without Meaning*. Kentfield, CA: Joseph Campbell Foundation, 2013.

Cameron, Julia. *The Artist's Way: A Spiritual Path to Higher Creativity*. NY: Penguin Putnam Inc., 2002.

Csíkszentmihályi, Mihály. *Flow: The Psychology of Optimal Experience*. New York: Harper and Row, 1990.

Csíkszentmihályi, Mihály. *Creativity: Flow and the Psychology of Discovery and Invention*. New York: Harper Perennial, 1996.

Ravindrakumar, Dave. *Psychomotor levels in Developing and Writing Behavioral Objectives*. R.J. Armstrong, ed. Tucson, Arizona: Educational Innovators Press, 1970.

Dewey, John. *Art As Experience*. NY: G.P. Putnam's Sons, 1934.

Dobbs, Stephen. *The DBAE Handbook: An Overview of Discipline-Based Art Education*. Santa Monica, CA: The J.P. Getty Trust, 1992.

Dorn, Charles. *Assessing Expressive Learning*. London: Lawrence Erlbaum Associates Publishers, 2004.

Douglas, Katherine and Jaquith, Diane. Engaging *Learners through Art Making: Choice-Based Art Education in the Classroom*. NY: Teachers College Press, 2009.

Dweck, Carol. *Mindset*. NY: Ballantine Books, 2007.

Edwards, Betty. *Drawing on the Right Side of the Brain*. NY: Tarcher, 1979.

Eisner, Elliot. *The Arts and the Creation of Mind,* New Haven and London: Yale University Press, 2002.

Erikson, Erik. *Childhood and Society*. W.W. Norton & Co. Inc.: 1950.

Erikson, Erik and Erikson, Joan. *The Life Cycle Completed*. NY: W.W. Norton & Co. Inc., 1997.

Fleming, Stephen. "The Power of Reflection: Insight into Our Own Thoughts, or Metacognition, Is Key to Higher Achievement in All Domains." *Scientific American*. September/October 2014, pp. 31-37.

Fletcher, Richard and Hattie, John. (2011). *Intelligence and Intelligence Testing 1st Edition*. NY: Routledge, 2011.

Freire, Paulo. *Pedagogy of the Oppressed*. NY: Continuum, 1993.

Fullan, Michael. *Leading in a Culture of Change*. San Francisco: Joseph Bass, 2007.

Gardner, Howard. *Frames of Mind: The Theory of Multiple Intelligences*. New York: Basic Books, 1983.

Gardner, Howard. *Multiple Intelligences: The Theory in Practice*. NY: Basic Books, division of HarperCollins Publishers Inc., 1993.

Genç, Erhan, et al. "Interhemispheric Connections Shape Subjective Experience of Bistable Motion." *Current Biology*, 2011 Sep 13;21(17):1494-9. Doi:10.1016/j.cub2011.08.003. Epub 2011 Sep 1. PMID: 21885284.

Genn, Robert. *Love Letters to Art*. Vancouver, Canada: Studio Beckett Publications, 2010.

Giffin, Mary and Felsenthal, Carol. *A Cry for Help*. Garden City, NY.: Doubleday &Co. Inc., 1983.

Gilligan, Carol. *In a Different Voice: Psychological Theory and Women's Development*. Cambridge, MA: Harvard University Press, 1982.

Goldstein, Kurt. *The Organism*. NY, NY: American Book Company, 1939.

Goleman, Daniel. *Emotional Intelligence: Why It Can Matter More Than IQ*, NY: Bantam Books, 1995.

Greene, Ross. *Lost at School*. NY: Scribner, division of Simon & Schuster, Inc., 2008.

Hammond, Zaretta. *Culturally Responsive Teaching and the Brain: Promoting Authentic Engagement and Rigor among Culturally and Linguistically Diverse Students*. CA: Corwin, Sage Co., 2015.

Handy, Charles. *The Age of Unreason*. Harvard Business Review Press, 1991.

Horney, Karen. *Neurosis and Human Growth*. NY: W.W. Norton & Co, Inc., 1950.

Hunter, Madeline C. *Mastery Teaching*. Corwin Press, Thousand Oaks, CA: Corwin Press, 1982.

Ibram, Kendi. *Stamped from the Beginning: The Definitive History of Racist Ideas in America*. NY: Nation Books, 2016.

Jenson, Eric. *Arts with the Brain in Mind*, Association for Supervision and Curriculum Development: Alexandria, VA, 2001.

Jensen, Eric. *Brain-based Learning: The New Paradigm of Teaching*. Thousand Oaks, CA: Corwin Press, 2008.

Kellaghan, Thomas, et al. *The Effects of Standardized Testing*. Boston/The Hague/London: Kluwer-Nijhoff Publishing, 1982.

Klein, Alyson. "No Child Left Behind: An Overview." *Education Week*, Bethesda, MD: April, 2015.

Kohn, Alfie. The Schools *Our Children Deserve: Moving Beyond Traditional Classrooms and "Tougher Standards."* NY: Houghton Mifflin Co., 1999.

Kohn, Alfie. *The Case Against Standardized Testing: Raising the Scores, Ruining the Schools*. Portsmouth, N.H.: Heinemann, 2000.

Krathwohl, David. "A Revision of Bloom's Taxonomy: An Overview." *Theory and Practice*, 2002, 41(4), 212-218.

Langer, Suzanne. Feeling and Form: *A Theory of Art Developed from Philosophy in a New Key.* Macmillan Pub. Co., 1955.

Lent, Robert W., Brown, Stephen D., & Hackett, Gail. "Toward a unifying social cognitive theory of career and academic interest, choice, and performance" [Monograph]. *Journal of Vocational Behavior*, 1994 (45): 79-122.

Levine, Peter. *The Cycle of Life: Creating Smooth Passages in Every Life Season.* Ukiah, CA: The Nourishing Company, 2007.

Lowenfeld, Victor. *Creative and Mental Growth.* NY: Macmillan Co., 1947.

Marsh, Herbert W. and Martin Andrew J. *Academic self-concept and academic achievement: relations and causal ordering.* British Journal of Educational Psychology March 2011;81(Pt 1):59-77.

Marzano, Robert et al. *Dimensions of Thinking: A Framework for Curriculum and Instruction.* Alexandria, Va.: Association for Supervision and Curriculum Development, 1988.

May, Wanda. "Student Responses to Media: Implications for Elementary Art Curriculum." *Studies in Art Education*, 1987;28(2), 105-117.

Merrow, John. *Addicted to Reform: A 12-Step Program to Rescue Public Education.* NY: The New Press, 2017.

Multon, Karen D., Brown, Stephen D., & Lent, Robert W. Relation of self-efficacy beliefs to academic outcomes: A meta-analytic investigation. *Journal of Counseling Psychology*, 1991 (38): 30-38. Doi: 10.1037//0022-0167.38.1.30

O'Donnell, Jane and Saker, Ann. "Teen Suicide is Soaring." *USA Today*. March 19, 2018.

O'Meara, Jodi. *RTI with Differentiated Instruction Grades 6-8, A Classroom Teacher's Guide*, Thousand Oaks, CA: Corwin: Sage Co., 2011.

Pariser, David. "Normal and Unusual Aspects of Artistic Development in the Juvenilia of Klee, Toulouse-Lautrec and Picasso." Paper presented at the Biennial Meeting of the *Society for Research in Child Development*, Kansas City, MO: 1989.

Piaget, Jean and Inhelder, Barbel. *The Child's Conception of Space*. London: Routledge & Kegan Paul, 1956.

Phillips, Lisa. *The Artistic Edge: 7 Skills Children Need to Succeed in an Increasingly Right Brain World*. Toronto, ON: Canada's Academy of Stage and Studio Arts, 2012.

Pinker, Steven. *Language as an Adaptation to the Cognitive Niche*. Oxford, NY: Oxford Univ. Press, 2003.

Pinkola Estes, Clarissa. *The Creative Fire: Myths and Stories on the Cycles of Creativity*. Louisville, CO: Sounds True, Inc. 2009.

Pipher, Mary. *Reviving Ophelia: Saving the Selves of Adolescent Girls*. NY: Ballantine Books, division of Random House Inc., 1994.

Ravitch, Diane. *Reign of Error: The Privatization Movement and the Danger to America's Public Schools*. NY: Random House, 2013.

Rop Gertjan. et al. "Task Experience as a Boundary Condition for the Negative Effects of Irrelevant Information on Learning" *Educ. Psychology* Rev DOI 10.1007/s10648-016-9388-9, 2016.

Root-Bernstein, Robert and Michelle. *Sparks of Genius: The Thirteen Thinking Tools of the World's Most Creative People*. Houghton Mifflin Co., NY, 1999.

Schaefer-Simmern, Henry. *The Unfolding of Artistic Activity: Its Basis, Processes and Implications*. University of California Press, Berkley and Los Angeles, 1948.

Schunk, Dale H. & Pajares, Frank. "Self-efficacy theory." In K. R. Wentzel & A. Wigfield (Eds.), *Handbook of Motivation at School* (pp. 35-53). New York, NY: Routledge, 2009.

Shearer, C. Branton. *The MIDAS: Professional Manual*. Kent, Ohio: MI Research and Consulting, Inc., 1996

Shearer, C. Branton. *The MIDAS handbook: Common Miracles in Your School*. Kent, OH: MI Research and Consulting, Inc., 2013.

Singer, Steven. *Middle School Suicides Double As Common Core Testing Intensifies*. Common Dreams, July 24, 2017.

Sousa, David A. *How the Brain Learns*. 3rd Ed. Thousand Oaks, CA: Corwin Press, 2006.

Sperry, Roger W. "Lateral Specialization of Cerebral Function in the Surgically Separated Hemispheres" in McGuigan F. et al. eds. *The Psychophysiology of Thinking*. NY: Academic Press, 1973.

Stankov, Lazar, Morony, Suzanne & Lee, Yim Ping. "Confidence: The best noncognitive predictor of academic achievement?" *Educational Psychology: An International Journal of Experimental Educational Psychology*. 2014, 34(1): 9-28.

Storr, Anthony. *The Essential Jung*. Princeton, N.J.: Princeton University Press, 1983.

Superville, Denisa. "Students Take Too Many Redundant Tests, Study Finds" *Education Week*, October 24, 2015.

Tate, Marcia L. *Worksheets Don't Grow Dendrites: 20 Instructional Strategies That Engage the Brain*. Thousand Oaks, CA: Corwin Press, 2003.

Tinajero, Carolina and Paramo, M. Fernanda. "Field dependence-independence cognitive style and academic achievement: A review of research and theory" *European Journal of Psychology of Education*. 1998;13(2):227-251.

Tomlinson, Carol and McTighe, Jay. *Integrating Differentiated Instruction and Understanding by Design*: Connecting Content and Kids. Alexandria, VA: Association for Supervision and Curriculum Development, 2006.

Urhahne, Detlef and Wijnia, Lisette. "Theories of Motivation in Education: an Integrative Framework." *Educational Psychology Review*. 2023; 35, 45.

Vansteenkiste, Martin, et al. *Motivating learning, performance, and persistence: the synergistic effects of intrinsic goal contents and autonomy-supportive contexts.* J. Pers.Soc.Psychol. 2004 (87): 246-260.

Vygotsky, Lev. *Mind in Society.* Cambridge, MA: Harvard University Press, 1978.

Walker Sydney. *Teaching Meaning in Artmaking.* Worcester, MA: Davis Publications, Inc., 2001.

Wiggins Grant and McTighe Jay. *Understanding by Design.* Columbus, OH.: Merrill Education/ Prentice Hall, Inc., 1998.

Wolfe Pat. *Brain Matters: Translating Research into Classroom Practice.* Alexandria, VA. Association for Supervision and Curriculum Development, 2001.

Zacarian, Debbie; Alvarez-Ortiz Lourdes; Haynes, Judie. Teaching to Strengths: *Supporting Students Living with Traum, Violence, and Chronic Stress.* Alexandria, VA. Association for Supervision and Curriculum Development, 2017.

Zohar Danah and Marshall Ian. *Spiritual Intelligence: The Ultimate Intelligence.* Edinburgh, UK: Bloomsbury Publishing, 2006.

WEBSITES

Brown, Brené. Daring Classrooms. SXSWedu 2017. YouTube. April 7, 2017. https://www.youtube.com/watch?v=DVD8YRgA-ck.

Brown University, Open Curriculum. https://www.brown.edu/academics/undergraduate/open-curriculum

"CASEL'S SEL Framework." *Collaborating Academic, Social and Emotional Learning.* Chicago IL. 1994. https://casel.org/wp-content/uploads/2020/12/CASEL-SEL-Framework-11.2020.pdf

"Common Core State Standards." Council of Chief State School Officers. http://www.corestandards.org/

"Every Student Succeeds Act (ESSA)." US Department of Education. https://www.ed.gov/essa?src=rn

"Fundamentals of SEL." *Collaborating Academic, Social and Emotional Learning.* Chicago IL. 1994. https://casel.org/what-is-sel/.

Genn, Robert. "Developing Ideas." The Painters Keys Newsletter, Canada: August 6, 2004. https://painterskeys.com/develop_ideas/.

"Graduation Requirements." Wisconsin Department of Public Instruction. https://dpi.wi.gov/graduation/requirements.

Klein, Alyson. "No Child Left Behind: An Overview." *Education Week*, Bethesda, MD: April, 2015. http://www.edweek.org/policy/politics/no-child-left-behind-an-overview/2015/04

Hinton, Kristen. *Aperture Education*, LLC. Ft. Mill, S. Carolina. 2016. www.apertureed.com.

Marshall, Ann. "PRISM--Pittsburgh's Research Based Instructional Supervisory Model for Staff Development." *PRISM.* 1982. http://eric.ed.gov/?id=ED251904.

McKenzie, Walter. "Multiple Intelligences Inventory." *Surfaquarium*. 1999. http://surfaquarium.com/MI/inventory.htm.

National Center for Education Statistics. "About NAEP: A Common Measure of Student Achievement," *Institute of Education Sciences*, Washington, D.C. August 16, 2023. http://nces.ed.gov/nations reportcard/about.

Priestly, Paul. *Support Artist in School*. YouTube. Feb 15, 2018. https://www.youtube.com/watch?v=xm5Jz 2Im5-o

Shearer, Branton. *MIDAS*. 1987. https://www.miresearch.org

Singer, Steven. "Middle School Suicides Double As Common Core Testing Intensifies." *Common Dreams*. March 7, 2017. https://www.commondreams.org/views/2017/07/24/middle-school-suicides-double-common-core-testing-intensifies

World Health Organization. Geneva, Switzerland. 2021. www.who.int

ABOUT THE AUTHOR

Marlene Rellinger Chapin is a twice National Board Certified Teacher in EAYA (Early Adolescent/ Young Adulthood Art). During her thirty-year career, Marlene has taught pre-school, elementary, middle, high school and undergraduate classes in art education. The author's unique and inclusive viewpoint reflects her experience in urban, rural and suburban schools in Ohio, Pennsylvania and Wisconsin.

PRISM, the *Pittsburgh Research-Based Instructional Supervisory Model*, was instrumental in forming the author's theory and practice while teaching at Brookline Elementary Teacher Center in Pittsburgh, PA. In addition, Chagrin Falls Exempted Village School District in Ohio and the Janesville School District in Wisconsin provided her the opportunities to develop Advanced Placement Studio Art and History of Art curricula. Additional resources can be found on her website *mcilluminations.com.*

Born and raised in Ottoville, Ohio, the author received her B.S. and M.A. in Art Education, respectively, at Bowling Green and Kent State Universities in Ohio. She currently is retired with her husband Dale on Lake Oconee in Georgia, much closer to grandchildren Noah, Madeline and Luca. Marlene can be contacted at mcilluminations@gmail.com.